"Isn't it an odd thing—that the d‹ tion than the resurrection of Jesu and scholar, is doing something al sive immersion, fifty days through meditation on Jesus's resurrection resurrection conversation."

D0379851

Eugene Peterson, Professor Emeritus of Spiritual Theology,
Regent College

"I just love good books on the resurrection of Jesus Christ! But so few of these texts ever take the time to carefully unpack exactly why this event is so absolutely incredible, or how it grounds virtually everything in the Christian life. However, Steve Mathewson's volume *Risen: 50 Reasons Why the Resurrection Changed Everything* remedies all that. The minute I saw it, I thought that this is exactly what we need. In fact, in the middle of a busy day I immediately dropped everything and studied the entire book in just a couple of hours. It is a very enlightening and rewarding read! I recommend it without hesitation."

Gary R. Habermas, Distinguished Research Professor,
Liberty University and Theological Seminary

"Without the resurrection of Jesus from the dead, our faith would be futile. I'm so grateful to Steve Mathewson for surveying God's Word to find fifty reasons for great celebration that Jesus was indeed raised to life on the third day. These reflections will deepen your faith in the God who still performs miracles, especially saving sinners from the death we deserved."

–Collin Hansen, editorial director, The Gospel Coalition;
co-author, *A God-Sized Vision: Revival Stories
That Stretch and Stir*

"The resurrection of Jesus is God's signed receipt that the death of Jesus is full payment for our sins. Yet, it means much, much more. Steve Mathewson has written a book of reflections on that momentous event that will leave you shouting, 'Jesus Christ has risen and what a difference that makes!'"

Haddon Robinson, Harold John Ockenga Professor
of Preaching, Gordon-Conwell Theological Seminary;
teacher on the *Discover the Word* radio program

"For too many Christians, resurrection is little more than a footnote to the sacrificial death of Jesus Christ, merely confirming that at Calvary the debt of sin was paid in full. Steve Mathewson has done us a great favor with his series of fifty expositions to lead us into the magnificent depths of this essential doctrine. As you work slowly and carefully through the meditations, you will understand why the Church has always asserted that the resurrection of Jesus Christ changes everything!"

Gerry Breshears, professor of theology, Western Seminary (Portland); co-author of *Vintage Jesus* and *Doctrine: What Christians Should Believe*

"A thought-provoking, spirit-stimulating exploration of a stunning—but strangely undervalued—reality. Steve's book isn't just for Easter. It's for life."

Barry Cooper, author and presenter of *Discipleship Explored*; co-author of *Christianity Explored*

"The power and purposes of Christ are wonderfully declared on every page of this book. Each chapter thoughtfully evokes and invites you to worship Jesus."

Pamela MacRae, assistant professor, Pastoral Studies Department, Moody Bible Institute

RISEN

50 REASONS WHY
THE RESURRECTION
CHANGED EVERYTHING

STEVEN D. MATHEWSON

BakerBooks

a division of Baker Publishing Group
Grand Rapids, Michigan

Published by Baker Books
a division of Baker Publishing Group
P.O. Box 6287, Grand Rapids, MI 49516-6287
www.bakerbooks.com

Printed in the United States of America

Library of Congress Cataloging-in-Publication Data
Mathewson, Steven D. (Steven Dale), 1961–
    Risen : 50 reasons why the resurrection changed everything / Steven D. Mathewson.
        p. cm.
    Includes bibliographical references.
    ISBN 978-0-8010-1514-4 (pbk.)
    1. Jesus Christ—Resurrection—Biblical teaching. 2. Apologetics. I. Title.
BT482.M28 2013
232'.5—dc23   2012028424

13 14 15 16 17 18 19   7 6 5 4 3 2 1

In keeping with biblical principles of creation stewardship, Baker Publishing Group advocates the responsible use of our natural resources. As a member of the Green Press Initiative, our company uses recycled paper when possible. The text paper of this book is composed in part of post-consumer waste.

green press INITIATIVE

To my children and their spouses

Erin and Manuel DeAnda
Anna and Grant Vander Ark
Benjamin and Nicole Mathewson
Luke Mathewson

Since, then, you have been raised with Christ, set your hearts on
things above, where Christ is, seated at the right hand of God.

Colossians 3:1

Contents

Foreword

Does it ever seem like Christians devote more attention to the cross than to the empty tomb? Churches that follow the historic, liturgical year often pay special attention to Lent, the forty days leading up to Good Friday and Easter weekend. Many people "give up" something for Lent, particularly certain kinds of food. The whole point of the season is to prepare spiritually for Christ's crucifixion.

Other denominations or congregations do not pay that much attention to the church calendar. After all, nothing in the Bible has established it; it's just a longstanding tradition. Still, many of these groups of believers in recent years have developed at least partial parallels to Lent, with forty days of focused study of some key topic appropriate to this time of year.

But what about the resurrection? There is little comparable to Lent for the fifty days between Easter and Pentecost. The church calendar does label each of the Sundays during this period as "The First Sunday after Easter," "The Second Sunday after Easter," and so on, but that's about it.

For all the theological debates about what Christ accomplished on the cross, and all the intricacies to the doctrines that were developed to answer this question, the resurrection seems to get short shrift in comparison. Christian teaching often focuses more on the question of the believability of the resurrection narratives than on their theological meaning. This is an important topic, to be sure, but not the most central one in most of the Scripture's teaching on the topic.

Why not take the fifty days after Easter, then, and embark on a simple yet profound study of the meaning of Jesus's resurrection? One can read any of the chapters in this book in as short a time as it takes to read the classic one- or two-page devotions in the booklets issued monthly that many families or individuals read at mealtimes or just before bed. One can also take the time to look up any or all of the Scriptures cited in each little chapter and turn that study into something considerably meatier.

Of course, nothing says you have to use this book just during late spring! It will enlighten and encourage you no matter what time of the year you take it up. Would you have guessed that the New Testament directly ties the resurrection into so many different matters—not only Christ's own person and work, but how we are saved, grow as Jesus's disciples, and look forward eventually to a glorious eternal state? It does, and Steve Mathewson makes it crystal clear.

Dr. Mathewson is already well-known among religious-book readers for his magnificent manual *The Art of Preaching Old Testament Narrative*, published by Baker Academic in 2002. He is well-known among preachers as an outstanding expositor of God's Word. He regularly contributes to such journals as *Leadership* and *Preaching Today*. Those who have attended the churches he has pastored know him as a wonderfully caring shepherd as well. Most recently, he has been the senior pastor of the Evangelical Free Church of Libertyville, Illinois, in the shadow of Trinity International University, with students and professors consistently in attendance. Even the most critically inclined of them recognize Steve's many gifts and his faithful, godly use of them.

Now Steve has gifted the world with this treasure trove of reflections on the resurrection. Take it, read it, savor it, and digest it. You'll be a better person for having done so.

Craig L. Blomberg
Distinguished Professor of New Testament
Denver Seminary, Littleton, Colorado

Introduction

The resurrection of Jesus Christ changes everything. It is the best possible news for human beings who live in a broken world and who enter that world separated from God because of their sin. In fact, the resurrection of Jesus Christ is one of his two massive accomplishments that together form the gospel or "good news." The apostle Paul makes this claim in the New Testament letter we identify as 1 Corinthians. He says that this gospel that saves people—the gospel that they received and believed, the gospel that he delivered to them as of first importance—consists of two elements (1 Cor. 15:3–4):

- "that Christ died for our sins"
- "that he was raised on the third day"

Both elements took place "according to the Scriptures," and both elements were witnessed in history.[1] The death of Christ was witnessed by his burial (v. 4). With one hundred pounds or so of spices and gummy substances encasing his body, and with a typical Palestinian rock-cut tomb requiring a stone weighing close to two thousand pounds to cover the entrance, it is farfetched to suppose that Jesus was not fully dead when he was buried. The circumstances surrounding a typical first-century burial in Jerusalem rule out any idea that Jesus had only passed out and somehow revived in the cool of the tomb, thus enabling his escape.

The resurrection of Jesus Christ was also witnessed in history by his appearance to more than five hundred people after he was raised to life (15:5–8). The sheer number of the witnesses and their backgrounds—at least one, James, was an unbeliever prior to seeing the resurrected Lord—testify to the reality of this event. In fact, when the apostle Paul wrote 1 Corinthians, most of these witnesses were still alive and thus available to be interviewed (v. 6).

Ironically, we often pay less attention to the resurrection than to the death of Christ. We glory in the cross of Christ, as we should (Gal. 6:14). But we give scant attention to the resurrection until Easter Sunday approaches.

This little volume, I pray, will correct this problem and will put you on a soul-stirring journey to explore the way the resurrection of Jesus Christ changes everything. It will show you how the resurrection converges with some tremendous biblical themes: the new covenant, the new heart we have received, and the new heaven and earth. It will show you how the resurrection of Jesus Christ shapes your present existence. This is a critical area of exploration because the "New Atheists" and the "New Gnostics" proclaim alternative worldviews for people in search of meaning.

New Atheists like Richard Dawkins and Christopher Hitchens flatly deny the metaphysical ("beyond the physical") claims of Christianity.[2] Hitchens even tries to portray Christians as confused about the nature of the resurrection body. He writes: "To this day, Christians disagree as to whether the day of judgment will give you back the old wreck of a body that has already died on you, or will reequip you in some other form."[3] This is completely false. When our journey brings us to the great resurrection chapter, 1 Corinthians 15, we will see that the Bible is clear that we do not get back "the old wreck of a body" that was buried when we died.

New Gnostics embrace a metaphysical worldview that differs radically from biblical Christianity. Salvation from our problems stems from an inner knowing that supposedly provides an intimate connection to the souls of other beings. In this scheme, the body is simply "condensed awareness," and yoga or some form of meditation becomes the framework for this intimate, spiritual soul-connectedness that leads to a revolution in our relationships. Death is simply an opening into the spiritual realm. As you read this book, someone else is reading Eckhart Tolle's *A New Earth: Awakening to Your Life's Purpose*, a book Oprah Winfrey has popularized by including it as a selection in Oprah's Book Club. What humanity needs, claims Tolle, is a transformation of consciousness. This consciousness "can flow into what you do and spread into this world" through "three modalities in which you can align your life with the creative power of the universe"—acceptance, enjoyment, and enthusiasm.[4] No wonder Oprah Winfrey tells readers, "Get ready to be awakened."[5] Where does the resurrection fit in? It does not, at least not along the lines envisioned by the Bible. Deepak Chopra, writing in *Reinventing the Body, Resurrecting the Soul: How to Create a New You*, denies the physicality of the body, arguing that "your physical body is a fiction."[6]

But Scripture presents a much different vision for our spiritual bodies and grounds this vision in the future bodily resurrection of Jesus's followers—a reality guaranteed by his own resurrection. In fact, the apostle Paul "speaks of the future resurrection as a major motive for treating our bodies properly in the present time (1 Cor. 6:14)."[7] Physicality is not diminished or denied but celebrated and brought into the realm of holiness. Yes, the resurrection of Jesus Christ changes the way we view and express our physicality in the present. It shapes our eternal existence. So it makes sense to set out on a journey through this little book and the Scripture passages it explores.

You can take your journey in one of two ways. First, you can read this volume like any other book. With only fifty brief chapters, it will not take you long to devour the contents and grasp how the resurrection changes everything. Second, you can read through this volume at the rate of one reading a day. Let each reason for Christ's resurrection fill your mind for the day. Reflect on the Scriptures that communicate each reason. You can begin any time of year, but the best day to get started is Easter Sunday. This is where the number fifty comes into play. I am not claiming that there are exactly fifty reasons why Christ was raised. There may be more, or there may be less, since many of these fifty reasons overlap. The biblical writers often look at the same reality from different angles. But the number fifty is ideal because anyone who reads a chapter a day beginning on Easter Sunday will complete the last reading on Pentecost Sunday—the day the church celebrates the coming of the Holy Spirit following Jesus's resurrection and ascension. Even if you or your church does not make much of the church calendar, I think you will agree that spending fifty days thinking about Jesus's resurrection will imprint this theme on your mind for the rest of your life.

Now, before we begin our fifty-chapter journey, we should consider briefly the meaning of *resurrection* and how it differs from other popular ideas about what happens to people when they die. Jesus's resurrection—and the promised resurrection of his followers—refers to a rising from the dead into a new kind of bodily existence not marred by sickness, aging, deterioration, or death.[8] Resurrection is more than resuscitation—coming back to life in the same kind of physical existence as before death. Resurrection is not disembodied existence, becoming an angel, or reincarnation.[9] Nor does the Bible teach annihilation—the view that you experience no life of any kind once you die but rather simply cease to exist. Resurrection, as we will see, involves a body. The immaterial part of believers, which continues to exist after death, is reunited with a new body.

All right, let the journey begin. Spend the next fifty chapters thinking deeply about the reasons why Jesus Christ was raised from the dead. When you are finished, I hope you will be moved and will join the church around the world in this joyful cry: "Christ is risen! He is risen indeed!"

To Give Us Eternal Life

> Jesus said to her, "I am the resurrection and the life. The one who believes in me will live, even though they die; and whoever lives by believing in me will never die. Do you believe this?" "Yes, Lord," she replied, "I believe that you are the Messiah, the Son of God, who is to come into the world."
>
> John 11:25–27

In the movie *Braveheart*, William Wallace got it right when he said, "Every man dies, not every man really lives."[1] Yes, this is a fact of life. Everyone dies. But not everyone truly lives. While you cannot change your appointment with death, you can ensure that you live before you die—and live after you die. Jesus is the one who makes this possible, because he is the resurrection and the life.

In John 10:10, Jesus makes this announcement about the impact his coming has on God's people: "I have come that they may have life, and have it to the full." This is in contrast to the religious leaders of Jesus's day, who sucked the life out of God's people by adding extra rules and regulations. Their intentions were noble. They offered these extra rules and regulations to help people obey God's Word. But the effect was just the opposite. They created a religion that stifled life. Jesus came to offer people eternal life (3:16). He defined eternal life as a relationship with God the Father and with Jesus himself (17:3). This life begins here and now, yet it extends throughout all eternity.

But how can anyone live forever when everyone dies? The answer is that Jesus is the resurrection and the life (11:25). In the New Testament, the term *resurrection* is a picture word. It literally means "standing up." It refers to a person's dead body being raised to new life. Most Jewish people in Jesus's day believed in a general resurrection of all people at some point in the future. What they did not anticipate, though, was that one person would be raised in advance of this general resurrection.[2] In John 11, Jesus demonstrates that he is the resurrection and the life by raising—or more precisely, resuscitating—his friend

Lazarus from death to life. This foreshadowed or anticipated Jesus's own death and resurrection, which he had already predicted (2:19–22).

At first, Jesus's claim sounds like a contradiction as he admits that believers will die and then claims that they will never die. However, in the first case, Jesus acknowledges physical death. Then, in the second, he acknowledges what comes after physical death. When believers in Jesus die physically, they immediately enter his presence (Luke 23:42–43; Phil. 1:21, 23). For a believer, to be absent from the body is to be present with the Lord (2 Cor. 5:8). Now this is life after death, but it is *not* resurrection. The dead in Christ still await resurrection, when their spirit or immaterial part of themselves is reunited with their bodies. Human beings were made to live in bodies. One day, believers in Jesus will experience bodily resurrection to live in the presence of God on a restored earth. This is "life after life after death!"[3]

To believe in Jesus, then, is to choose life *before* we die and *after* we die. Jesus is the one who connects us to the presence of God. Without God, all we have is the empty print and trace of the true happiness that the human race lost when it rebelled against God. French mathematician and philosopher Blaise Pascal argues that people try in vain to fill this empty print and trace with everything around them. However, "none can help, since this infinite abyss can be filled only with an infinite and immutable object; in other words by God himself."[4] The psalmist simply says of God:

> In Your presence is perfect joy;
> Delights are ever in Your right hand. (Ps. 16:11 NJPS)

As we will discover, the resurrection of Jesus provides for us a new quality of life right here and right now (Col. 3:17). But this life is not over when we die. Yes, we will all die. But, "we know that the one who raised the Lord Jesus from the dead will also raise us with Jesus and present us . . . to himself" (2 Cor. 4:14).

To Show His Power over Death

> But God raised him from the dead, freeing him from the agony of death, because it was impossible for death to keep its hold on him.
>
> Acts 2:24
>
> For we know that since Christ was raised from the dead, he cannot die again; death no longer has mastery over him.
>
> Romans 6:9

Toward the end of my wife's pregnancy with twins, her obstetrician left for a week of vacation. "Don't worry," the doctor told her, "it's unlikely that these babies will arrive before I return." Two days before her doctor returned, my wife went into labor. There was no way she could hold back little Anna and Ben. The apostle Peter uses this image to make a key point about Jesus's resurrection, declaring that death could not hold on to Jesus any more than a pregnant woman can hold her unborn child in her body.

In the very first sermon recorded in the Acts of the apostles, Peter describes God's act of raising Jesus from the dead as "freeing him from the agony of death" (Acts 2:24). The word *agony* is literally the expression "labor pain." What a remarkable picture. Death is in labor and is unable to hold back its child, the Messiah. To emphasize this point, Peter then adds: "because it was impossible for death to keep its hold on him." Why was this impossible? The answer is that God made Jesus both Lord and Christ (v. 36). As Lord, Jesus is to be identified with *Yahweh*, the personal name for God used in the Old Testament (Ps. 110:1, which Peter quotes in Acts 2:34–35). Jesus is also to be identified as the Messiah (Christ), the Anointed One who would deliver God's people by leading them out of bondage. No wonder death could not keep its hold on Jesus!

The apostle Paul makes a similar point in Romans 6:9, emphasizing that, as a result of Jesus's resurrection, Jesus cannot die again. Think about the difference between Jesus Christ's resurrection and the resurrection of Lazarus. Douglas Moo writes: "Unlike Lazarus's 'resurrection' (better, 'revivification'), which did not spare him from another physical death, Christ's resurrection meant a decisive and final break with death and all its power."[1] To make sure we get the point that Jesus cannot die again, Paul restates this for emphasis: "death no longer has mastery over him" (v. 9).

Notice that the emphasis here is on Jesus. *He* cannot die again. Death no longer has mastery over *him*. But what difference does this make for us, Jesus's followers? When you follow the apostle Paul's argument in Romans 6, you find that our union with Christ—that is, our connection to him—makes this true for us as well. In fact, verse 9 is connected grammatically to verse 8, which says: "Now if we died with Christ, we believe that we will also live with him."

But how are we united to Christ? This union or connection to Christ comes through faith (Rom. 1:17; 3:22, 25–26; 4:5; 5:1). Peter makes the same point at the end of his sermon in Acts 2, calling people to repentance (a turning from sin to God) and baptism (a sign of belonging to the people of God) in the name of Jesus Christ for the forgiveness of sins (Acts 2:38–39).

So then, Jesus's victory over death is a victory in which we share when we are united with him. What a comfort this is when we face the sting of death. I will never forget the day I helped a funeral director place the bodies of three teenage boys in their caskets. These three young men and their driver's education instructor died in a tragic car accident. The funeral director had taken so much care preparing the bodies that he was short on time and needed help before the boys' families arrived for the viewing. I felt tremendous sorrow as I helped lift the boys' lifeless bodies into their caskets. But I found comfort in the knowledge that each one of the boys and their instructor had placed their faith in the Lord Jesus Christ. All four were—and are—connected to him. All four will be raised to new bodily life. Because of our connection to Jesus Christ, the one who died and rose from death, we can be confident that death will one day have no mastery over us. Hold on to that encouragement the next time death confronts you.

Jesus was raised from death . . .   **3**

To Heal Us

> Then know this, you and all the people of Israel: It is by the name of
> Jesus Christ of Nazareth, whom you crucified but whom God raised
> from the dead, that this man stands before you healed.
>
> Acts 4:10

I cannot imagine better news than learning that a cure has been found
for cancer, heart disease, cystic fibrosis, and clinical depression. The
truth is, there is a cure. One of the great benefits of the death and
resurrection of Jesus Christ is our healing. Acts 3 tells the story of the
apostle Peter healing a beggar who was lame from birth. Peter and
John encountered this man as they were about to enter the temple to
pray. He asked them for money. But Peter said: "Silver or gold I do
not have, but what I do have I give you. In the name of Jesus Christ
of Nazareth, walk" (Acts 3:6). Peter took the man by the hand and
helped him up, and the man's ankles and feet instantly became strong.
The man walked and jumped and praised God.

Peter then tells the astonished crowd that the power for this miracle
came from the God who glorified Jesus by raising him from the dead
(vv. 12–15). Then Peter adds: "By faith in the name of Jesus, this man
whom you see and know was made strong. It is Jesus' name and the
faith that comes through him that has completely healed him, as you
can all see" (v. 16). So it is through faith in Jesus that healing begins.
Peter then reiterates this in Acts 4:10, after he and John were jailed
for proclaiming in Jesus the resurrection of the dead, and were subse-
quently questioned about the source of power and authority behind
the lame man's healing.

There are two key points to keep in mind about the healing Jesus
provided through his death and resurrection. First, while this healing
includes physical healing, it involves much more. The term *healed* in
Acts 4:10 means "whole, well, healthy." In the statement Peter makes
immediately prior to this, the term *healed* is actually another Greek
term that means "saved" (v. 9; see also v. 12). So the healing to which

19

Peter refers in Acts 4:10 is healing from all the effects of sin. It is healing from the physical, emotional, legal, relational, and spiritual consequences of sin.

The second key point has to do with when this happens. If Jesus's death and resurrection really provide for our healing, then why do some Christians struggle with depression and emotional pain? Why do some Christians need wheelchairs or dialysis or chemotherapy? The answer is found in Peter's sermon in Acts 3, and it is the second point we need to keep in mind about healing.

In Acts 3:19–21, Peter talks about "times of refreshing" and "the time for God to restore everything." Christians will experience complete healing when the time comes for God to restore everything. Until then, we live in the times of refreshing. The healing process has begun. But we should not assume from the healing of the lame beggar that every last person who trusts in Jesus during this age will receive complete physical healing now. Sometimes God will allow us to struggle with physical or emotional wounds in order to show us that his grace is sufficient (2 Cor. 12:7–11). My godly grandmother was only fifty-eight years old when she died three months after being diagnosed with cancer. But through all our struggles with emotional and physical illness, we can have confidence that the God who has begun the healing process will bring it to completion through the name of Jesus Christ of Nazareth, whom God raised from the dead. Through the death and resurrection of Jesus, God has healed us "already but not yet." Thank God that he has started the process, and that complete healing will eventually come.

Jesus was raised from death . . .

4

To Receive the Blessings Promised to David

> God raised him from the dead so that he will never be subject to decay. As God has said, "I will give you the holy and sure blessings promised to David."
>
> Acts 13:34

I have a friend whose company occasionally receives complimentary tickets to sporting events from one of their clients. A few years ago, my friend gave me a couple of these tickets—two courtside seats in the United Center to watch the Chicago Bulls play the Philadelphia 76ers. My son Luke and I had better seats than some of the celebrities in the crowd sitting *behind* us! My friend's blessing resulted in me being blessed. Sometimes, we are most blessed when someone else is blessed. That's the case with the resurrection of Jesus Christ. We are blessed because the resurrection enabled him to receive the blessings promised to David.

King David holds a special place in the storyline of the Bible. After God removed Israel's first king, Saul, from office, he made David Israel's king and even described him as "a man after my own heart" who "will do everything I want him to do" (Acts 13:20–22). From David's descendants, God brought his people the Savior Jesus (v. 23). The apostle Paul reviewed this fact when he offered a word of encouragement one day in a synagogue during one of his mission trips. According to Acts 13:34, he made the point that the words of Isaiah the prophet, "I will give you the holy and sure blessings promised to David" (Isaiah 55:3), anticipated the resurrection of Jesus.

The logic is this: Jesus is the descendant of David who will receive the blessings and fulfill the promises made to David. Since death makes it impossible for him to receive these blessings and fulfill the promises, God had to raise Jesus from death!

But what exactly are the blessings God promised David? One aspect of the blessing is the resurrection itself. Like Peter at Pentecost (Acts 2:27), Paul quotes Psalm 16 as an anticipation of the resurrection

(Acts 13:35). In Psalm 16:10, David wrote: "You will not let your holy one see decay." The argument is that David could not possibly be referring to himself. After all, he died, was buried, and his body decomposed (Acts 13:36). The one God raised from the dead who does not see decay is clearly someone else (v. 37).

This leads to the second aspect of the blessing. In 2 Samuel 7:12–16, God promised to raise up a dynasty through David—a dynasty through which God would establish an everlasting kingdom. While verses 12–15 refer to Solomon, verse 16 expands the promise by saying: "Your house and your kingdom will endure forever before me; your throne will be established forever." This can simply mean that a descendant of David would always occupy the throne.

Yet Isaiah the prophet expands the promise even further. In a remarkable prophecy, Isaiah argues that God will replace his people's gloom with glory, their darkness with light (Isa. 9:1–3). In Isaiah's day, the gloom and darkness came from oppression by the Assyrian empire. How would God bring light into this darkness? The answer is that he would decisively defeat Israel's enemy (v. 4). But how would he defeat the enemy? The answer is that he would end war altogether (v. 5). But how would he end war altogether? The stunning answer is that God would do this through the birth of a child—a child who would rule and would be called "Wonderful Counselor, Mighty God, Everlasting Father, Prince of Peace" (v. 6). Amazing! This child would possess all the qualities that people in the ancient Near East looked for in a king—a counselor, a mighty warrior, a father, and a prince who had the authority to rule. This child would also be divine—one who is truly wonderful, who exists as God, who is everlasting, and whose rule brings peace. Then, Isaiah informs us that this child "will reign on David's throne and over his kingdom . . . from that time on and forever" (v. 7).

The resurrection of Jesus makes possible the eternal rule of a righteous, powerful king in the line of David who will bring peace—a life in which everything is whole, complete, and exactly right. This encourages us when our lives seems fragmented, unfulfilling, and frustrating. Our longing for relief, for security, for wholeness, and for peace will be satisfied in the rule of David's offspring, King Jesus, who was raised from death to life.

To Forgive Our Sins

> But the one whom God raised from the dead did not see decay. There-
> fore, my friends, I want you to know that through Jesus the forgiveness
> of sins is proclaimed to you.
>
> Acts 13:37–38

> And if Christ has not been raised, your faith is futile; you are still in
> your sins.
>
> 1 Corinthians 15:17

The words of a well-known hymn capture the sheer joy of knowing
that God is not counting our sins against us when we are connected
to his Son, Jesus Christ:

> My sin—O, the bliss of this glorious thought,
> My sin—not in part but the whole
> Is nailed to the cross and I bear it no more,
> Praise the Lord, praise the Lord, O my soul![1]

What may surprise us is the role Jesus's resurrection plays in the
forgiveness of our sins. We are used to thinking about Jesus's death
as the basis for our forgiveness. After all, Ephesians 1:7 says about
Jesus Christ: "In him we have redemption through his blood, the
forgiveness of sins." Similarly, Hebrews 9:22 claims that "without the
shedding of blood there is no forgiveness." The Scripture is quite clear
that Jesus Christ died for our sins as our substitute, taking on himself
the penalty that we deserved (Rom. 5:8; Heb. 9:15; 1 Pet. 2:24; 3:18).

Yet the apostle Paul, in his sermon recorded in Acts 13, proclaims
the forgiveness of sins as a result of Jesus's resurrection. The term
therefore at the beginning of Acts 13:38 establishes this connection.
Similarly, in 1 Corinthians 15:17 Paul makes it clear that we are still
in our sins if Christ has not been raised. So while the death and resurrection of Jesus Christ were separate events, they are inseparable
elements when it comes to providing forgiveness for our sins. After

all, the gospel, or good news, consists of two elements. First, Christ died for our sins (v. 3). Second, Christ was raised on the third day (v. 4). Both events happened according to the Scriptures, and both had historical confirmation. Jesus's burial confirmed his death, and his appearance to eyewitnesses confirmed his resurrection. It is this gospel in which we stand for our salvation (vv. 1–2).

But why do we need forgiveness? The answer in one word is *sin*. When sin entered the world through the rebellion of the first human beings, it separated humans from God the Creator, cutting us off from God's life-giving presence. It placed us under a death sentence. Romans 5:16 describes it like this: "The judgment followed one sin and brought condemnation." But by the gospel—Jesus's death and resurrection—we are saved (1 Cor. 15:2).

Salvation is God's act of saving (or delivering or rescuing) us from our sin and from all the problems our sin has created. One of the huge aspects of this salvation is *forgiveness*. This term, as it is used in the New Testament, refers to letting go or releasing something. When God forgives us, he releases us from the penalty we deserve. God has the right to exact that penalty. In fact, he must exact that penalty in order to be just. For God to look the other way would be as unjust as a judge excusing convicted murderers or rapists from the penalty they deserve. But through the death and resurrection of Jesus, God satisfies the demands of his justice. The penalty is paid, and so God is able to release us from his personal right to exact the penalty for our offense.

Clearly, Jesus's death provides the grounds for forgiveness. It provides payment of the penalty. The New Testament does not spell out quite as clearly how the resurrection provides forgiveness. But if forgiveness comes through Jesus, as Acts 13:37 insists, then he must be risen for there to be any power or authority for issuing forgiveness. Both his death *and* resurrection are needed for God to forgive sinners.

The resurrection, then, gives us hope when we sin. To be sure, we are not supposed to sin as followers of Jesus Christ (1 John 1:5–6; 3:6, 9–10). But the fact is, Christ-followers still sin (1:8–10). When we fail and fall into lying, cheating, lusting, gossiping, stealing, or coveting, we can be confident that Jesus's resurrection provides the power and authority for God to be faithful and just, to forgive our sins, and to purify us from all unrighteousness.

Jesus was raised from death . . . 6

To Elevate His Power and Authority

> And who through the Spirit of holiness was appointed the Son of God
> in power by his resurrection from the dead: Jesus Christ our Lord.
>
> Romans 1:4

Suppose you are writing a letter to a group of Christians who need to
understand what God has done about their problem with sin. Where
would you begin as you describe the gospel, the good news about what
God has done through Christ? The apostle Paul's majestic presentation
of the gospel in his letter to the Romans begins with the resurrection.
The gospel to which Paul has been set apart (Rom. 1:1–2) centers on
Jesus the Messiah. This is the point of Paul's reference to Jesus as
"his Son, who as to his earthly life was a descendant of David" (v. 3).
Jesus is the Anointed One, a king in the line of David who would
reign forever (2 Sam. 7:12–16). Romans 1:4 then announces that this
Messiah-King was appointed to a new and even more powerful position by his resurrection from the dead!

To understand Paul's argument, we must carefully consider his
words. The term translated *appointed* is used consistently throughout
the New Testament to mean "appoint, determine, fix."[1] Through the
resurrection, then, Jesus was designated or appointed "the Son of
God in power." The expression "in power" might describe the verb,
meaning that the declaration or designation was done with power.
But it is more likely that the expression "in power" modifies the words
it immediately follows in the Greek text: "Son of God." Finally, Paul
reveals the identity of the one designated "the Son of God in power."
It is Jesus the Christ (Messiah) who is also "our Lord."

However, saying that Jesus was *appointed* Son of God sounds like
the heresy of Adoptionism, a view from the second century AD that
denied the eternal sonship of Jesus. According to this view, Jesus was
not the Son until he was adopted at his baptism or at his resurrection. But Paul is saying something much different when he declares

25

that Jesus was "appointed [to be] the Son of God in power by his resurrection from the dead" (v. 4). He is not describing a change in *essence* but a change in *status*. The exact wording of Romans 1:3 assumes the preexistence of the Son of God—"who became from the seed of David."[2] This recalls the apostle John's statement that "the Word became flesh" (John 1:14). So, God has designated Jesus to be the Son of God in a new way at his resurrection. Through the resurrection, Jesus is exalted to a greater level of power and authority than he previously had.

Douglas Moo explains this well: "The transition from v. 3 to v. 4, then, is not a transition from a human messiah to a divine Son of God (Adoptionism) but from the Son as Messiah to the Son as both Messiah *and* powerful, reigning Lord."[3] This is consistent with the apostle Peter's conclusion about Jesus, the one whom God raised from death (Acts 2:32). Peter concludes: "Therefore let all Israel be assured of this: God has made this Jesus, whom you crucified, both Lord and Messiah" (v. 36).

Notice that the instrument of this designation is the "Spirit of holiness" (Rom. 1:4)—certainly a reference to the Holy Spirit who, Paul says elsewhere, "raised Jesus from the dead" (8:11). So a new age of salvation has begun! In this age, Jesus reigns as the Son of God who is both Messiah and Lord.

Like millions of others, I have an account on Facebook, the social network that has taken the culture by storm. My friends and I use our "status" on our Facebook page to tell others why we are excited. We are about to become parents, or better yet, grandparents. Our volleyball team won the district championship. The forecast for the second week of October is for sun and seventy-degree temperatures—a cause for joy if you live in Chicago or Montana. But the one reason for excitement that outdoes all others is that King Jesus has been appointed to a new and even more powerful position by his resurrection. His reign as Messiah-King means salvation from life's deepest problem (sin) for all those who believe. Yes, thanks to the resurrection, the gospel *is* the power of God for salvation to all who believe. Put that as your status!

To Justify Sinners

> The words "it was credited to him" were written not for him alone, but also for us, to whom God will credit righteousness—for us who believe in him who raised Jesus our Lord from the dead. He was delivered over to death for our sins and was raised to life for our justification.
>
> Romans 4:23–25

> Through him everyone who believes is set free from every sin, a justification you were not able to obtain under the law of Moses.
>
> Acts 13:39

I was born with a deficiency that is far more serious than iron deficiency or vitamin A deficiency or even AIDS—Acquired Immune Deficiency Syndrome. My deficiency is deadly. You were born with it too. It is a righteousness deficiency. We have acquired it—along with every other person in the human race (Rom. 1:18–3:19)—because of the sin of Adam, the first member of the human race (5:12–14). This means we are all condemned people, guilty before God.

But thank God there is a solution! The solution is God's gift of righteousness—a right status before God as a result of God's saving activity through Jesus Christ. It turns out that Jesus's resurrection is a key part of this solution. Let's explore how this solution works.

The place to begin is Romans 3:21–26. This paragraph of Scripture makes three key points about God's righteousness. First, it comes solely through faith in Jesus Christ (v. 22). Second, this righteousness is needed by everyone (vv. 22–23). Third, this righteousness comes in the form of a legal declaration of acquittal from all charges brought against us because of our sin (v. 24). *Justification* is the word that refers to this legal declaration of acquittal. Amazingly, this judicial verdict, which Jewish theology said was not available until the last judgment, is given the moment a person believes. It is a verdict motivated solely by God's grace—that is, his undeserved, unmerited favor.

But on what basis is God able to do all of this? What makes it possible for this to happen? According to Romans 3:24–26, justification is possible through the death of Jesus Christ. However, Romans 4:25 presents both the death and the resurrection of Jesus as the cause of our justification. In Romans 4, the apostle Paul presents Abraham's faith as a model of faith for both Jews and Gentiles. According to Genesis 15:6, Abraham, the father of the Jewish nation, exercised faith in God, and God credited righteousness to Abraham. In the same way, God does this for those today who "believe in him who raised Jesus our Lord from the dead" (Rom. 4:24). It is unusual for Paul to mention God as the object of faith rather than Jesus Christ. But he does this to make a strong parallel between Abraham's faith and our faith. Both Abraham's faith in God and our faith in the God who raised Jesus from the dead result in God crediting to us the gift of right standing. The basis for this is both the death and resurrection of Jesus Christ. Paul uses the same preposition—"for" or "because of"—before both. Similarly, when Paul taught at the synagogue in Antioch in Pisidia, his statement that "through him everyone who believes is set free from every sin" (Acts 13:39) flowed out of his teaching on Jesus's resurrection (vv. 32–38).

While Jesus's death made justification possible by paying for our sins (Rom. 4:25), turning aside God's righteous anger against sin, and satisfying God's justice (3:25–26), Jesus's resurrection confirms that our justification has been secured. It vindicates Jesus and verifies he has defeated sin (6:9–10). Jesus's resurrection gives us confidence that God's plan to give us a right standing through faith in Christ has worked.

What a difference this makes in our daily outlook on life. If we belong to God through faith in Christ, we do not have to wonder if God is angry with us. There is no reason to worry that God might count our sins against us. So remember Jesus's resurrection when your mind gets bombarded with negative thoughts about God not accepting us because we do not measure up to his standards. Jesus's resurrection changes everything. It gives us confidence that we have been freed from the penalty we deserve for both our past and future sins.

To Give Us a New Way to Live

We were therefore buried with him through baptism into death in order that, just as Christ was raised from the dead through the glory of the Father, we too may live a new life.

Romans 6:4

Now if we died with Christ, we believe that we will also live with him. For we know that since Christ was raised from the dead, he cannot die again; death no longer has mastery over him. The death he died, he died to sin once for all; but the life he lives, he lives to God. In the same way, count yourselves dead to sin but alive to God in Christ Jesus.

Romans 6:8–11

Do you ever wish you could start over with your life? Do you ever wish you could change your identify? The good news is that if you are united with Christ, then you are not the old person you used to be. You are new and alive because of Christ's resurrection. The good news, according to Romans 6:4, is that "just as Christ was raised from the dead through the glory of the Father, we too may live a new life." Literally, that last line reads: "we too may walk in newness of life." The basis for this, according to verses 5–8, is our union with Christ an incredible concept we will discuss in the next chapter.

But what does it mean to walk in newness of life? Our experience will be like Christ's experience in two ways. First, we will share in Christ's resurrection and thus share in his defeat of death. Paul's verb "will live" in verse 8 suggests that this experience is a future reality for us. "But this future life of resurrection casts its shadow into the believer's present experience."[1] So we are also affected in our present reality. According to verse 10, the second way we walk in newness of life is to live life "to God." That is, we live life for the glory of God.

Now when Paul says in verse 10 that Christ "died to sin once for all," he is not implying that Christ ever sinned. Rather, as a man who lived in the old age, Christ was subject to the power of sin even though

29

he never gave in to it. But as a result of dying to sin, Christ lives to God—and so do we as a result of our union with Christ!

Paul is not content to end his discussion here, as if this is some kind of abstract concept. Rather, he tells us that being raised to walk in newness of life should make a huge difference in our lives, and he offers us two strategies. The first, in verse 11, is to consider or take into account our new identity, the fact that we are dead to sin and alive to God. The second strategy, in verses 12–14, is to live out this new identity by choosing God over sin.

Two pictures help us wrap our minds around what it means to choose God over sin. First, we are not to let sin rule as a king whom we are obligated to obey (v. 12). Second, we are not to offer the "members" of our body to sin as weapons of wickedness but to God as weapons of righteousness (v. 13). The term *members* includes our abilities and desires as well as the parts of our physical body. So we use our words, our imaginations, our sexuality, our ability to reason, and our physical strength for the glory of God. As N. T. Wright correctly observes, Paul's argument "is not simply that there are two ways to live, and that one must choose between them; it is that the baptized have changed their ground, and must learn to behave according to the territory they now find themselves in."[2] Because we have life through the resurrection of Christ, we choose God as the one in whom we are satisfied and delighted (Ps. 16:10–11). A recent song by Jason Gray, "I Am New," affirms that a new life and identity are not just a dream for Christ's people. Instead of being defined by mistakes we have made, we are being remade in the image of Christ.

Thank God for the new identity and the new desires we possess because he raised his Son, Jesus, from death to life!

To Unite Us with Him in His Resurrection

For if we have been united with him in a death like his, we will certainly also be united with him in a resurrection like his. For we know that our old self was crucified with him so that the body ruled by sin might be done away with, that we should no longer be slaves to sin—because anyone who has died has been set free from sin. Now if we died with Christ, we believe that we will also live with him.

Romans 6:5–8

When Tim Smith was eleven years old, he made a life-changing discovery. He was snooping in his mom's closet, looking for Christmas presents, when he stumbled across his birth certificate and discovered that his biological father was major league baseball pitcher Tug Mc-Graw. Eventually, Tim was reunited with his biological father, and that connection made a huge difference in the direction his life took. When Tim wanted to drop out of college to hit the road as a musician, Tug provided the financial support to make it possible. Eleven Grammy Awards and ten Country Music Association Awards later, Tim Mc-Graw's success can be traced back to his connection to Tug McGraw.

Similarly, believers in Christ can trace the privileges they enjoy to their union with Christ. It is by being united with Christ in his death and resurrection that we experience the blessings of the gospel. Simply put, union with Christ refers to the inseparable connection we have with Christ. The New Testament speaks both of believers being "in Christ" (Rom. 6:11; 8:1; Eph. 1:3–4) and of Christ being "in" believers (Rom. 8:10; 2 Cor. 13:5; Col. 1:27). This union happens at our conversion to Christ. This is clear from Romans 6:3 where Paul speaks of being "baptized into Christ Jesus." Why does Paul mention water baptism here when he speaks so consistently and insistently in Romans about the role of faith? The answer is that it makes sense for Paul to use water baptism to stand for conversion, because baptism portrays the death, burial, and resurrection we experience in Christ.

Now, what is there to celebrate about this union? Romans 6:5–8 highlights two particular blessings. The first is the result of being united to the likeness of Christ's death. According to Romans 6:6–7, the "old self"—the person we used to be in Adam—died so that we do not have to pursue a sin-dominated life. The purpose of this crucifixion was to render powerless our "body ruled by sin." For Paul, a "body" is a person turned outward in action. So he uses the expression "body ruled by sin" to refer to a person dominated by sin. The ultimate purpose of our "old self" being crucified with Christ is to free us from slavery to sin. Paul elaborates on this idea in Romans 6:15–23.

The second blessing of our union with Christ relates specifically to being united with Christ in his resurrection. The result is experiencing life with him. The "if-then" structure in Romans 6:5 signals that our union with Christ in his death assures our union with Christ in his resurrection. To take this one step further, "if we died with Christ, we believe that we will also live with him" (v. 8). Some understand this statement to be a reference to our present experience in which we live in Christ's resurrection power and in the new spiritual reality it has provided (Eph. 2:6; Col. 3:1). Others interpret it as a reference to our future bodily resurrection (Rom. 8:11). So which is it? Perhaps we should view this as a "both-and" rather than an "either-or." Certainly, Paul has our future bodily resurrection in mind because he argues elsewhere with those who view the resurrection as an already accomplished reality (2 Tim. 2:18). Yet Paul works backward from this future event and views believers as having been raised to new life in Christ in the present (Col. 3:1).

Because we have been united with Christ in his resurrection, as well as in his death, life will never be the same—in the future *and* in the present. We "have a whole new existence that we need to be celebrating."[1] So celebrate this new life whenever you feel discouraged about your present circumstances. Celebrate it when you find your life disappointing and when things do not turn out the way you expected or dreamed. Celebrate that God raised Jesus from death so that you could be united with Jesus in his resurrection.

Risen

Jesus was raised from death . . . **10**

To Make Us Fruitful

> So, my brothers and sisters, you also died to the law through the body of Christ, that you might belong to another, to him who was raised from the dead, in order that we might bear fruit for God.
>
> Romans 7:4

I want my life to count. I want my life to make a difference for the kingdom of God. I want my life to produce what is good and pleasing, like the fruit produced by a fruit tree. I assume you want the same for your life too. Thankfully, the resurrection of Jesus Christ makes this possible. Without the resurrection, God's people would not be free to bear fruit for God. The problem is our relationship to the law of Moses. Originally, the law of Moses was a gracious gift from God given to a redeemed community to help them live the good life in the land God gifted to them. But as we learn in Paul's letter to the Romans, the law has another function. It reveals the depth of our sinfulness (3:20). So, trying to keep the law to gain right standing with God is a dead end. Verse 20 affirms: "no one will be declared righteous in God's sight by the works of the law." Instead, the law brings wrath (4:15).

So how do we escape the condemnation we receive from the law? The only way this can happen is for us to die to the law, because "the law has authority over someone only as long as that person lives" (7:1). Paul illustrates this by reminding us how "by law a married woman is bound to her husband as long as he is alive, but if her husband dies, she is released from the law that binds her to him" (v. 2). The death of her husband, then, frees her to marry another man without being an adulteress (v. 3).

In verse 4, Paul draws his conclusion: believers in Christ have died to the law as their spouse, and so are free to "remarry" Christ. Now this conclusion has troubled many Bible students over the years. It does not flow easily from the illustration in Romans 7:2–3. The illustration would make more sense if the law of Moses had died. Then

33

God's people, the widowed spouse, would be free to marry Christ. It seems ridiculous to think in terms of a dead spouse getting remarried! But this is precisely Paul's point. Believers in Christ have experienced death because they have been incorporated into Christ's death. The expression "body of Christ" here refers not to the church but to the physical body of Christ, which bore our sins on the cross (1 Pet. 2:24). So our union with Christ is in view again.

But it is the statement about Christ's resurrection that resolves the tension over the seemingly absurd idea that we, as believers in Christ, are dead people who remarry another spouse. Believers in Christ who are united with him in his death are also united with him in his resurrection. "It is as if the Holy Spirit reproduces Jesus's death and resurrection in our lives when we believe in Christ."[1] This, of course, changes everything! According to Thomas Schreiner:

> Romans 7:4 indicates that the death and resurrection of Christ not only were designed to remove the condemnation of the law, but they also broke the power of the law, so that believers could live lives pleasing to God by bearing good fruit.[2]

Because of Jesus's death and resurrection, we now "serve in the new way of the Spirit" (Rom. 7:6) in fulfillment of God's promise to give his people a new heart and put his Spirit within them (Ezek. 26:25–27). With the power of the resurrection flowing into our lives, we can now bear fruit for God. This fruit may come in the form of people who find new life in Christ because we shared the gospel with them. This fruit may consist of someone who has been able to overcome bitterness or drug addiction because we spent months or years showering them with God's love. Perhaps the fruit will be a new church we helped to establish or an established church we helped to revitalize because of faithful, Christlike living. It is our relationship with the One who was raised from the dead that makes all the difference.

To Give Life to Our Mortal Bodies

> And if the Spirit of him who raised Jesus from the dead is living in you, he who raised Christ from the dead will also give life to your mortal bodies because of his Spirit who lives in you.
>
> Romans 8:11

Due to the ravages of sin, our bodies are constantly decaying. Elbows get tendonitis. Hips wear out. Eyesight diminishes. Arthritis attacks our joints. Hearing fades. Eventually, our bodily systems shut down and usher in death. The grim reality is that all human beings have mortal bodies. Even if you live longer than most people and reach one hundred years of age, you will still not escape death. Romans 8:10 provides a ray of hope: "But if Christ is in you, then even though your body is subject to death because of sin, the Spirit gives life because of righteousness." But exactly how does the Spirit give life? The thrilling answer is future bodily resurrection! "He who raised Christ from the dead will also give life to your mortal bodies because of his Spirit" (v. 11). Amazing! Our bodies will be raised to life just as Jesus's body was raised to life. This will be accomplished by God himself, through his Spirit who now lives in us. "The Spirit, here as throughout Paul's thought, is the *present* guarantee of the *future* inheritance, and of the body which will be appropriate for that new world."[1]

As Christians, we must be as clear as the apostle Paul on the nature of our future resurrection. Like Jesus's resurrection, ours will involve our physical bodies being raised to life. The Scriptures do not teach existence as disembodied spirits as in ancient Greek thought. Greek philosophers such as Plato and Cicero taught that at death the soul was released from the "prison-house" of the body, as if the body was a bad thing. It is true that believers in Jesus will spend some time after death apart from our bodies. Scripture indicates that we will spend this intermediate state—between our physical death and our bodily resurrection—in the presence of Jesus (2 Cor. 5:8). In Philippians 1:23, Paul says that for a believer to "depart"—that is, to die—is to "be with Christ." Jesus said to the thief on the cross who expressed his trust in Jesus: "Truly I tell you, today you will be with me in paradise" (Luke 23:43).

Now Scripture does not explain how this works, whether the immaterial part of us receives a temporary body or simply exists apart from a body. Regardless, the intermediate state is a place of conscious rest in the presence of Christ where we await the resurrection of our bodies. So, living as disembodied spirits is not what Scripture means by resurrection. Nor does Scripture teach that we become angels—another popular view in contemporary culture.

Furthermore, resurrection is not reincarnation as taught in Hinduism and other eastern religions. According to Hebrews 9:27, "people are destined to die once, and after that to face judgment." Scripture does not teach that people who die come back as ants or lions or humans in an unending cycle of birth and rebirth until reaching Nirvana, a state where all desire and feeling are gone. No, our physical bodies will be raised to join the immaterial part of us that resides after death in the presence of Christ. The idea of resurrection also rules out annihilationism, the view that a person has no future existence of any kind after death.

God made human beings to experience life through bodily existence. He gave us noses to smell lilacs, eyes to view sunsets, fingers to play piano keys, arms to hug loved ones, toes to wiggle in wet sand, ears to hear songbirds, and legs to climb mountains. For believers in Jesus, death is not the end of bodily existence. We can look forward to the day when God's Spirit gives life to our mortal bodies so that we can run and talk and hear and taste in the new earth—God's restored creation.

12

To End Our Obligation
to the Flesh

> Therefore, brothers and sisters, we have an obligation—but it is not to
> the flesh, to live according to it. For if you live according to the flesh,
> you will die; but if by the Spirit you put to death the misdeeds of the
> body, you will live.
>
> Romans 8:12–13

Toward the end of Mark Twain's classic novel *Tom Sawyer*, one of the
main characters, Huckleberry Finn, turns up missing. Life had changed
dramatically for Huck. He had stumbled onto a fortune and saved the
life of Widow Douglas. Out of her gratitude, Widow Douglas took
him into her home, cleaned him up, clothed him, educated him, and
taught him manners. Huck received a new life. But then he vanished.
Townspeople searched everywhere, even combing the river. Finally, Tom
Sawyer went poking around some old hog sheds behind an abandoned
slaughterhouse and found Huck lying unkempt, uncombed, and clad in
tattered clothes. He had returned to his old way of life, back to where
he thought he wanted to be. Like Huck, we are constantly attracted to
the old way of life. It tries to lure us away from our new life and back
into slavery to sin. But the resurrection of Jesus changes everything.

The term *therefore* at the beginning of Romans 8:12 signals an
important consequence or outcome of Jesus's resurrection and our
future resurrection that was discussed in verse 11. The consequence
or outcome is that we are no longer debtors who are obligated to
live according to the flesh. The apostle Paul uses the term *flesh* here
as a metaphor for our orientation to rebellion against God. It is our
tendency to sin. Even though our "old self" was crucified with Christ
so that we are no longer the people we used to be (6:6–7), there is still
a residue of sinfulness with which we struggle as long as we live on
earth in its present age—in the age, or old realm, of sin and death.

But because of our life in the Spirit—the Spirit who raised Jesus
from the dead—we are no longer obligated to live according to the

flesh. It is no longer our master, even though we may lapse from time to time into old patterns of behavior and give in to this old master.

This is precisely what Romans 8:13 tells us not to do. It calls us to "put to death the misdeeds of the body" so that we will live. What exactly are the misdeeds of the body? These are the actions done through our body under the influence of the flesh; that is, under the influence of our tendency to fall back into sin. In Galatians 5:19–21, Paul explains:

> The acts of the flesh are obvious: sexual immorality, impurity and debauchery; idolatry and witchcraft; hatred, discord, jealousy, fits of rage, selfish ambition, dissensions, factions and envy; drunkenness, orgies, and the like. I warn you, as I did before, that those who live like this will not inherit the kingdom of God.

Paul's warning at the end of this passage resembles his statement in Romans 8:13 that those who live according to the flesh will die. While Christians never escape the struggle with the flesh in this life and will, from time to time, lapse back into sin, a lifestyle marked by the flesh indicates that a person does not belong to Christ and will not inherit the kingdom of God. Our lifestyle reflects the realm to which we belong—the old realm of sin and death or the new realm of the Spirit. Those who belong to the new realm of the Spirit who raised Jesus from the dead will put to death the misdeeds of the body and experience life.

Romans 8:13 captures an important balance between God's role and our role. Right living is not achieved through our unaided effort (what we would label moralism or legalism). Nor are we simply passive believers who "let go and let God." Rather, we do our part in putting to death the misdeeds of the body through the power of the Spirit, who lives within us and will one day give life to our mortal bodies just as he gave life to Jesus's mortal body three days after his crucifixion.

To Provide Us with Future Glory

I consider that our present sufferings are not worth comparing with
the glory that will be revealed in us.

Romans 8:18

C. S. Lewis speaks of an "inconsolable secret" that resides in every
human being. It is "a desire for something that has never actually
appeared in our experience."[1] Certain books or music or memories
arouse this longing. For me, it is the memory of the first time I kissed
the girlfriend who became my wife. It is hearing Percy Faith's recording
of "A Summer Place." It is the photo of my brothers and me standing
on the summit of Long's Peak in Colorado. It is the smell of alfalfa
and the memory of baling hay on my grandparents' farm in Penn-
sylvania when I was a boy. But Lewis argues that these are "only the
scent of a flower we have not found, the echo of a tune we have not
heard, news from a country we have never yet visited."[2] The reality is,
these things point forward to our future glory—a future glory made
possible by the hope of resurrection. The apostle Paul talks about this
when he writes, "I consider that our present sufferings are not worth
comparing with the glory that will be revealed in us" (Rom. 8:18).

The expression "present sufferings" refers to any kind of suffering
we face in this fallen world, including persecution and ridicule for following Christ, cancer, heart disease, depression, sexual abuse, broken
relationships, financial problems, hunger, unemployment, rejection,
disappointment, loneliness, lack of fulfillment, the death of a spouse
or child or parent or friend, and even our own death.

Amazingly, the apostle Paul claims that these sufferings "are not
worth comparing" with future glory. He is calling us to look at suffering with a "long view" that takes in the future glory brought about
by the resurrection. We need to hear this because the temptation is
to look at suffering with a "short view." If we are not careful, we can
even interpret God by our present sufferings. We can conclude that
God does not care or is not powerful because of what we face in our

present existence. But when we factor in the resurrection of Jesus and our future resurrection, it completely changes our perspective!

"We must," Paul suggests, "weigh suffering in the balance with the glory that is the final state of every believer"—a glory that is so wonderful that "suffering flies in the air as if it had no weight at all."[3] Paul makes the same point in 2 Corinthians 4:17: "For our light and momentary troubles are achieving for us an eternal glory that far outweighs them all."

What is this glory that will be revealed in us? It is certainly our future life in the new heaven and new earth promised in the Old Testament! In Isaiah 65:17–19, God promises:

> See, I will create
>   new heavens and a new earth.
> The former things will not be remembered,
>   nor will they come to mind.
> But be glad and rejoice forever
>   in what I will create,
> for I will create Jerusalem to be a delight
>   and its people a joy.
> I will rejoice over Jerusalem
>   and take delight in my people;
> the sound of weeping and of crying
>   will be heard in it no more.

Paul seems to allude to this in Romans 8:21 when he says that "the creation itself will be liberated from its bondage to decay and brought into the freedom and glory of the children of God." The wonder is that this glory "will be revealed in us" (v. 18). So we will not share in creation's glory as much as creation will share in our glory.

I need this perspective to encourage me when I face disappointment and heartache. As C. S. Lewis observes, "the leaves of the New Testament are rustling with the rumor that it will not always be so."[4] Yes, and it is more than a rumor. Our future glory is certain because God's Spirit will one day give life to our mortal bodies—just as he raised Jesus from death—so that our present suffering will give way to a life of glory in God's new heaven and earth!

Jesus was raised from death . . . **14**

To Set Creation Free
from Its Bondage

> That the creation itself will be liberated from its bondage to decay and brought into the freedom and glory of the children of God. We know that the whole creation has been groaning as in the pains of childbirth right up to the present time.
>
> Romans 8:21–22

Creation is currently in a state of bondage to decay. This explains why we have floods, hurricanes, tornadoes, tsunamis, famines, bubonic plague, shark attacks, bear attacks, and drought. Romans 8:20 explains: "For the creation was subjected to frustration, not by its own choice, but by the will of the one who subjected it, in hope." So who subjected creation to frustration? The most likely answer is God. God is the one who decreed the curse as a judgment on sin (Gen. 3:17).

But God's act of subjecting the creation to frustration was actually positive. It was done "in hope." Romans 8:21–22 describes this hope, explaining that "the creation will itself will be liberated from its bondage to decay and brought into the freedom and glory of the children of God." This is why "the creation waits in eager expectation for the children of God to be revealed" (v. 19). This revealing, or unveiling, of the true nature of those people who belong to God's family takes place at our future resurrection. It is possible because of Jesus's resurrection and the future resurrection of his followers (v. 11).

However, this perspective seems at odds with the description of the "day of the Lord" in 2 Peter 3:

> The heavens will disappear with a roar; the elements will be destroyed by fire, and the earth and everything done in it will be laid bare. . . . That day will bring about the destruction of the heavens by fire, and the elements will melt in the heat. But in keeping with his promise we are looking forward to a new heaven and a new earth, where righteousness dwells. (vv. 10, 12–13)

41

Some Christians have concluded from this passage that the earth will be completely destroyed—burned up—and that God will create a different earth. Second Peter 3:10–13, though, is describing purification, not annihilation. Its language, at least in part, comes from Old Testament descriptions of a refining process—that is, purification by fire. Most importantly, this destruction resembles the destruction of the flood (vv. 6–7). Obviously, the flood did not obliterate or remove the earth. It simply purged it. When the flood waters subsided, the ark did not land on a different planet but on the same earth. So final judgment will be like the flood judgment. The earth will still exist, but in a radically transformed state. The new heaven and earth will be a place where "righteousness dwells" (v. 13). Paul describes this same end result in Romans 8:21 as "the freedom and glory of the children of God."

I need this encouragement as I weep for families in Alabama who recently lost loved ones in a devastating tornado. I need this encouragement as I pray for my relatives in New Jersey who are bracing for a hurricane that may destroy their home. I need this encouragement when I recall how a furious blizzard disoriented a friend of mine while he was hunting in the mountains of Montana a few years ago. My friend ended up wandering for miles, losing both his strength and eventually his life. This is not how life is supposed to be. Isaac Watts captures our longing for what God has promised to do as a result of the resurrection of Jesus Christ:

> No more let sins and sorrows grow,
> Nor thorns infest the ground;
> He comes to make His blessings flow
> Far as the curse is found,
> Far as the curse is found,
> Far as, far as, the curse is found.[1]

Yes, Christ's resurrection has set in motion a series of events that will culminate in creation being set free from its bondage to decay. Thanks to Christ's resurrection, God's blessings will flow over creation as far as the curse is found.

To Adopt Us into God's Family

> Not only so, but we ourselves, who have the firstfruits of the Spirit, groan inwardly as we wait eagerly for our adoption to sonship, the redemption of our bodies.
>
> Romans 8:23

Like creation groans (Rom. 8:20 22), human beings groan inwardly under the stress of bondage to decay. The frustration and pain of living in decaying bodies in a decaying world sometimes seems to be more than we can tolerate. Relationships fall apart. Chronic pain intensifies. Disappointments multiply. Cancer spreads. Tragedy strikes. And so, our groaning increases. But like creation (v. 19), we also wait eagerly for deliverance. What we wait for eagerly is our adoption to sonship—something Paul describes in Romans 8:15.

When we think of adoption, we tend to think of parents adopting an infant whose biological parents are unable to nurture them and provide the necessary care due to their circumstances. For example, my daughter-in-law, Nicole, was adopted by wonderful Christian parents when she was three months old. But in the first-century Greek-Roman world, an adopted son was usually an adult. Often, wealthy people without offspring adopted heirs to whom they could pass on their estates and all the wealth that went with it. Adoption conferred on these heirs all the legal rights and privileges a biological child would have.

Here are two important clarifications. First, the adoption image in Romans 8 applies to God's sons and daughters even though adopted heirs in the Greek-Roman world were male. This is clear from the way that the Old Testament uses sonship to refer to the nation of Israel as a whole, irrespective of gender.[1] Second, the adoption in Romans 8 is both "already" (v. 15) and "not yet" (v. 23). What, then, is the future or "not yet" aspect of this adoption? The answer involves "the redemption of our bodies." This is a reference to God's promise to "give life to your mortal bodies" (v. 11)—that is, to raise us from the dead just as Christ was raised from death!

When Romans 8:23 is read in its context, it is obvious that what we are longing for is an earthly existence in God's restored creation. Although believers in Jesus go to heaven when they die, they will not stay there. What they have to look forward to is life on a restored earth. If our life in Christ's presence between death and resurrection is "life after death," then our resurrection life is "life after life after death!" So when the pain and pressure of our present existence builds, let us remember our adoption into God's family through Christ—an adoption that leads to the redemption of our bodies.

Imagine what kind of life we will have when our bodies are redeemed along with the entire creation. Life will be full of beauty, intimacy, and adventure. We will never again feel anxious, depressed, afraid, bored, ashamed, or unfulfilled. We will not have to worry about car accidents or cancer taking our lives. We will not have to deal with flu, arthritis, cavities, chronic fatigue, bad cholesterol, or heart attacks. Work will not drain or frustrate us.

It is reasonable and realistic for us to wait eagerly for this kind of life because we have "the firstfruits of the Spirit." This is a farming metaphor. Just as the first ears of corn or melons guarantee a larger harvest to come, so the presence of God's Spirit as the first installment of God's salvation guarantees that more is coming. According to Romans 8:15, we have already been adopted. Two specific blessings are attached to this. The first is intimacy, a blessing evidenced by the privilege we have of addressing God as our father. The second blessing is inheritance. We are "heirs of God and co-heirs with Christ" (vv. 16–17). The "not yet" part of our inheritance is our coming life in resurrected bodies on the new earth that God restores. When that part of our existence arrives, the bad times will truly be over for good!

To Intercede for Us
at God's Right Hand

> Who then is the one who condemns? No one. Christ Jesus, who died—more than that, who was raised to life—is at the right hand of God and is also interceding for us.
>
> Romans 8:34

> Now there have been many of those priests, since death prevented them from continuing in office; but because Jesus lives forever, he has a permanent priesthood. Therefore he is able to save completely those who come to God through him, because he always lives to intercede for them.
>
> Hebrews 7:23–25

Jesus is praying for you! If Jesus had not been raised to life, he would be unable to intercede for us. But because he lives forever, he always lives to intercede for us. This is an even more wonderful blessing than we might imagine because Jesus is the one person who can condemn us and whose condemnation would stick. But instead of condemning us as Judge, he intercedes for us as High Priest.

In Romans 8:34, Paul is careful to note that the resurrected Christ Jesus, the one who intercedes for us, is "at the right hand of God." This is an allusion to Psalm 110:1 where King David writes: "The LORD says to my lord: 'Sit at my right hand until I make your enemies a footstool for your feet.'" In this statement, King David understands *his* Lord, or master, being elevated to a place of majesty and power by the LORD—Yahweh, the God of Israel. As the story of the Bible develops, we learn that Jesus the Messiah is David's Lord. So we have none other than the exalted Lord of glory interceding for us!

But what does it mean for Jesus to intercede for us? Three clues in Scripture provide the answer. First, during Jesus's last supper with his disciples, he said to Simon Peter: "Simon, Simon, Satan has asked to sift all of you as wheat. But I have prayed for you, Simon, that your faith may not fail" (Luke 22:31–32). We expect, then, that Jesus prays for each of us—his followers—that we will not fail. Jesus still does for us at the right hand of God what he did for Peter on earth.[1]

A second clue is the identification of Jesus as a priest in Hebrews 7:23–25. The writer of Hebrews has already explained what a priest, specifically a high priest, does:

> Every high priest is selected from among the people and is appointed to represent the people in matters related to God, to offer gifts and sacrifices for sins. He is able to deal gently with those who are ignorant and are going astray, since he himself is subject to weakness. (5:1–2)

A high priest, then, represents God's people in matters related to God. The high priest acts on behalf of God's people.

This leads to a third clue. Throughout the letter to the Hebrews, the author encourages his audience that Christ "is able to *help* those who are being tempted (2:18), and to provide mercy and grace to *help* them in their time of need (4:16)."[2]

From these clues, we conclude that Jesus prays for the gracious and merciful help we need whenever we are tempted. We may assume that Jesus's petitions for us "cover anything and everything that would prevent us from receiving the final salvation he has won for us at the cross."[3]

Like the old spiritual song says, I am desperately "standing in the need of prayer."

I need prayer to forgive and to avoid bitterness when someone wrongs me. I need prayer for boldness in sharing the gospel of Christ when it invites ridicule. I need prayer for perseverance when I get discouraged about a health issue or financial challenge that never seems to go away. I need prayer to avoid greed and envy when my friends have the money to remodel their kitchen and I do not. Thankfully, Jesus is praying for me and for all his followers. Just as the Spirit who raised Jesus from the dead intercedes for us (Rom. 8:26–27), the resurrected Christ himself intercedes for us, praying to God the Father on our behalf.

To Fulfill the Scriptures

> That he was raised on the third day according to the Scriptures.
>
> 1 Corinthians 15:4

> He said to them, "This is what I told you while I was still with you: Everything must be fulfilled that is written about me in the Law of Moses, the Prophets and the Psalms." Then he opened their minds so they could understand the Scriptures. He told them, "This is what is written: The Messiah will suffer and rise from the dead on the third day, and repentance for the forgiveness of sins will be preached in his name to all nations, beginning at Jerusalem."
>
> Luke 24:44–47

In J. R. R. Tolkien's story *The Two Towers*, Sam poses a rather profound question to his fellow hobbit Frodo. Both have encountered wonders and survived danger on their journey. Now, as they travel the perilous road to Mordor, Sam says, "I wonder what sort of a tale we've fallen into." Jesus did not need to ask this question. He clearly understood the tale into which he had fallen. After his resurrection, he explained to his followers that his death and his resurrection were part of the developing story of the Scriptures. The apostle Paul also saw Jesus's resurrection as an event in the story that the Scriptures had long anticipated.

The Scriptures to which Paul refers in 1 Corinthians 15:4 and to which Jesus refers in Luke 24:44–47 are what we call the Old Testament or what Jewish people today refer to as the Hebrew Bible, Jewish Bible, or the Tanakh.[1] We know this is the case because Jesus speaks of "the Law of Moses, the Prophets and the Psalms"—the very divisions of the Old Testament or Hebrew Bible (Luke 24:44).

Exactly how, then, did Jesus's resurrection fulfill the Scriptures? We must recognize that the term *fulfill* refers to more than mere predictions that literally take place at a later point in time. While it can have this meaning, *fulfill* often refers to the way in which a later event brings out the full significance of a previous statement, event, or prophecy.

Therefore, we need to be cautious about combing the Old Testament portion of the Scriptures to find precise predictions of Christ's resurrection. Rather, as N. T. Wright observes, the phrase "according to the Scriptures" in 1 Corinthians 15:4 "looks back to the scriptural narrative as a whole, not simply to a handful of proof-texts."[2] Certainly, the story Paul has in mind is the Old Testament's story of God forgiving Israel's sins, bringing in a new age, renewing the covenant, restoring creation, and raising his people from the dead (Ezek. 37).[3] Likewise, when Jesus describes "what is written" in terms of his suffering, resurrection, and the proclamation of repentance and forgiveness (Luke 24:46–7), he is not quoting a particular text or texts from the Hebrew Scriptures. Rather, he sees these events in his own life and ministry as anticipated by the Hebrew Scriptures. On the road to Emmaus, he explained to a couple of his disciples "what was said in all the Scriptures concerning himself" (v. 27).

This is not to deny the existence of key texts in the Hebrew Scriptures that anticipate Jesus's resurrection. Paul, by mentioning Jesus being raised on the third day (1 Cor. 15:4), "may have found some typological significance in the third day reference to God's vindication of his people in such texts as Genesis 42:18, Exodus 19:16, Joshua 2:22, Ezra 8:32, Esther 5:1, Jonah 1:17 (cf. Matt. 12:40), and especially Hosea 6:2."[4] Peter, in his sermon at Pentecost (Acts 2:24–36), "saw the combined evidence of Psalms 16:8–11 and 110:1 as bearing witness to the Messiah's resurrection."[5] Imagine Jesus explaining to his disciples how God did not abandon him to the realm of the dead and how God did not let his holy one—Jesus!—see decay (Ps. 16:10). Imagine Jesus expounding on Isaiah's statement about the suffering servant and applying it to himself: "After he has suffered, he will see the light of life and be satisfied" (Isa. 53:11).

How encouraging to know that Jesus's resurrection stands in line with the great story of God working to redeem and restore his people to life in his presence, where true fullness and joy are found. This is the tale into which we, as followers of Jesus, have fallen!

To Make Our Faith
and Preaching Worthwhile

> And if Christ has not been raised, our preaching is useless and so is your faith. More than that, we are then found to be false witnesses about God, for we have testified about God that he raised Christ from the dead. But he did not raise him if in fact the dead are not raised.
>
> 1 Corinthians 15:14–15

"Santa Claus Is Coming to Town" is a classic Christmas song. It is charming, entertaining, and even has a good moral lesson. Santa knows when you've been bad or good, the song claims, so be good for goodness' sake. However, the song is simply not true. Little boys and girls who work hard to maintain good behavior will not be showered with gifts from Santa. Sorry, Virginia, the Santa Claus of that song simply does not exist. The song may be entertaining and have some moral value, but it is definitely not good news. In fact, it is a rather useless message on which to build one's life.

Unfortunately, some folks treat the resurrection of Jesus like the idea of Santa Claus coming to town. In the first century, there was a group of people in the church in ancient Corinth who did not believe in a bodily resurrection. They did not agree that Jesus or anyone else could be raised to life. If they are right, says Paul, there are serious implications for our faith and our preaching. He argues: "And if Christ has not been raised, our preaching is useless and so is your faith" (1 Cor. 15:14). The term *useless* means "empty." So without the resurrection, the Christian faith—and our preaching of that faith—has no substance. It is as useless as a snowblower in Jamaica or a screen door on a submarine.[1]

Sometimes people claim that Christianity is still worth following even if it is not completely true. After all, it teaches people good morals that lead to a safer, peaceful, stable society. But Paul will have none of this. The usefulness of our faith and preaching rises or falls with the resurrection. He develops this in more detail in 1 Corinthians

49

15:14–19. In verse 15, he argues that without the resurrection, the Christian faith has no credibility. If Christ has not been raised, "we are then found to be false witnesses about God." By "we," Paul is referring to the apostles. They were to the church what the founding fathers—Washington, Adams, Jefferson, and Franklin—were to the United States of America. If the apostles are wrong about the resurrection, then their overall message cannot be trusted.

Furthermore, Paul argues that without the resurrection, the Christian faith has no victory. Here the consequences start to get more personal. Paul puts it bluntly in verse 17: "And if Christ has not been raised, your faith is futile; you are still in your sins." If you are still in your sins, then there is no possibility of the life change described throughout the New Testament and even in 1 Corinthians (6:9–11). Without the resurrection, there would be no power available for life transformation (Phil. 3:10).

Finally, Paul argues that without the resurrection, the Christian faith has no future. In 1 Corinthians 15:18, he says: "Then those also who have fallen asleep in Christ are lost." "Fallen asleep" is simply a euphemism for death—just like the expression "passed away" is a softer way to refer to death in our culture. Paul does not buy into the idea that at death the soul sheds the body and is, in effect, released from prison. Human beings were meant for bodily existence. Without the resurrection, the dead in Christ are lost. They have no future.

Incredibly, some preachers are content to preach about the resurrection of Christ while denying that it actually happened in history. They view the gospel accounts as simply describing a "spiritual event" of some kind in which "the 'stone' of legalism has been rolled away, and the 'risen body,' the true spark of life and identity hidden inside each of us, can burst forth."[2] Such preaching, though, is not worthwhile. If the story is fiction rather than fact, then we have no reason to preach it as good news.

But keep preaching. Keep believing. "Christ indeed has been raised from the dead," affirms Paul in 1 Corinthians 15:20. Our preaching and our faith have substance, credibility, victory, and a glorious future!

To Guarantee
Our Future Resurrection

> But Christ has indeed been raised from the dead, the firstfruits of those who have fallen asleep. For since death came through a man, the resurrection of the dead comes also through a man. For as in Adam all die, so in Christ all will be made alive. But each in turn: Christ, the firstfruits; then, when he comes, those who belong to him.
>
> 1 Corinthians 15:20–23

> For we believe that Jesus died and rose again, and so we believe that God will bring with Jesus those who have fallen asleep in him.
>
> 1 Thessalonians 4:14

If you have ever planted a garden, you know the thrill of harvesting the first strawberries or tomatoes or ears of corn. These "firstfruits" guarantee that a larger harvest is coming. The resurrection of Jesus Christ functions this way. His resurrection is a "firstfruits" that signifies more resurrections are coming. Just as death came to all who are "in Adam," resurrection comes to all who are "in Christ." In 1 Corinthians 15:23, Paul is careful to spell out the order. First, Christ, the firstfruits, is raised. Then, when he comes, those who belong to him are raised. The time of our resurrection, then, is the return of Christ to earth—what we refer to as the "second coming."

First Corinthians 15:20–23 is a summary of Paul's teaching earlier in this magnificent chapter. So let's take a moment to review it. For Paul, the "good news," or gospel, of Jesus Christ consisted of two elements. The first element is that "Christ died for our sins" (v. 3), and the second element is that "he was raised on the third day" (v. 4). Paul summarizes the gospel with the same two events in 1 Thessalonians 4:14 when he writes: "We believe that Jesus died and rose again."

But how can we be so certain that these are the two key elements to the gospel when Paul mentions several other items, including the burial of Jesus, in the opening sentences of 1 Corinthians 15? The answer is the structure of Paul's argument. A closer look reveals that Paul makes two key points about each element—both the death and the resurrection of Christ:

1. Both were verified by the witness of Scripture.
2. Both were verified by the witness of history.

The mentions of the death and resurrection of Christ are both followed by the phrase, "according to the Scriptures." Then Paul shows that both the death and resurrection of Christ were verified in history. The verification for Christ's death was his burial. The details—the size of the rock covering the entrance, the presence of guards, the fact that the women saw where Jesus's body was placed (Luke 23:55)—make it impossible that the disciples stole his body, that the women had the wrong tomb, or that Jesus had simply passed out and revived in the cool of the tomb. The verification for Christ's resurrection is the company of witnesses who saw him after his resurrection. The sheer number and variety of those who saw the resurrected Christ is impressive. Numerically, Paul points to over five hundred witnesses, most of whom were still alive when he wrote his letter (1 Cor. 15:6). These witnesses included both men and women, the apostle Peter (Cephas), the Twelve, the rest of the apostles, and two unbelievers whose lives were changed. These two are James, certainly a reference to the half brother of the Lord, and Paul himself. James became a key leader in the church at Jerusalem (Acts 15:13; Gal. 1:15–19). Paul, of course, ended his career as a terrorist who persecuted the church and became an apostle (1 Cor. 15:9).

It is important to establish the truthfulness of Jesus's resurrection. Like the first tulip that blossoms in the early spring and anticipates an entire flower bed of color, Jesus's resurrection signals that more resurrections are on the way. This includes yours—if you belong by faith to Jesus!

20

To Destroy All Other Powers through His Reign

> Then the end will come, when he hands over the kingdom to God the Father after he has destroyed all dominion, authority and power. For he must reign until he has put all his enemies under his feet. The last enemy to be destroyed is death. For he "has put everything under his feet." Now when it says that "everything" has been put under him, it is clear that this does not include God himself, who put everything under Christ.
>
> 1 Corinthians 15:24–27

Dark spiritual forces cause us more trouble on a daily basis than we realize. To be sure, some folks go too far and try to exorcise demons of lust or greed when Scripture calls for no tactic of this sort when dealing with these sins. But the fact is demonic influence may lurk behind the disagreement you are having with your pastor or your parents. The apostle Paul claims that the problems we face in the church, problems that seem to be no more than human conflict, are really struggles we face with the rulers, authorities, and powers of this dark world (Eph. 6:12). Similarly, the idea that you have to live perfectly for God to accept you may well be demonic. The apostle Paul attributes certain legalistic approaches to deceiving spirits and demons (1 Tim. 4:1–3).

The good news is that through the bodily resurrection of Jesus Christ, these enemies have been defeated. Yes, the defeat of evil forces described in 1 Corinthians 15:24–27 flows out of the resurrection of Christ and the resulting resurrections of his followers (vv. 20–23). These resurrections occur at Jesus's second coming. "Then the end will come" (v. 24). The end arrives "when he hands over the kingdom to God the Father after he has destroyed all dominion, authority, and power" (v. 24). We will consider the enemy of death in the next chapter. But first, who exactly are the enemies to which 1 Corinthians 15:24 refers?

The identity of "all dominion, authority, and power" has been debated throughout church history. Some say these are earthly, human rulers as in 1 Corinthians 2:6–8 where Paul uses a word for "rulers" that is similar to the one he uses here in 15:24 for "dominion" (or "rule" in the ESV). Others argue that 1 Corinthians 15:24 refers to demonic rulers—angelic beings who have sided with the devil in rebellion against God. The reason for this is that these expressions are used by Paul in other letters to refer to demonic beings (Eph. 1:21; 3:10; 6:12; Col. 1:16; 2:10, 15). New Testament scholar Anthony Thiselton argues that the phrase "all dominion, authority, and power" includes "*any* kind of structural opposition to God, whether social, political, economic, ethical, spiritual, or even . . . 'supernatural.'"[1]

The best interpretation is to take the phrase "all dominion, authority, and power" as a reference to demonic powers, realizing that earthly rulers who act in violence and greed are simply expressions of the demonic powers behind them.[2] New Testament scholar Clinton Arnold points out that the apostle Paul has employed terms here that Jewish and pagan writers used in reference to evil spirits and invisible powers.[3] "They are the evil forces that have made their influence felt in every kind of human opposition to God and every form of structural evil."[4]

Because of his death and resurrection, Christ has begun his kingdom and rules as exalted Lord. When he returns, he will forever stop Satan and his forces from resisting God and God's people. Elsewhere, the apostle Paul tells us that we have the resources we need to stand against the schemes of Satan and his spiritual forces right now by virtue of our union with the resurrected Christ. In Ephesians 6:10–20, Paul uses the image of armor to help us remember these resources of truth, righteousness, peace, faith, salvation, and God's Word—all of which he discussed previously in Ephesians. We take this stand in confidence, knowing that Jesus in his resurrection struck the forces of darkness a fatal blow!

To Destroy the Enemy of Death

> The last enemy to be destroyed is death. . . . When the perishable has been clothed with the imperishable, and the mortal with immortality, then the saying that is written will come true: "Death has been swallowed up in victory." "Where, O death, is your victory? Where, O death, is your sting?" The sting of death is sin, and the power of sin is the law. But thanks be to God! He gives us the victory through our Lord Jesus Christ.
>
> 1 Corinthians 15:26, 54–57
>
> They can no longer die; for they are like the angels. They are God's children, since they are children of the resurrection.
>
> Jesus (Luke 20:36)

According to the Bible, death is an enemy. We need to hear this because popular culture tries to soften the sting of death by portraying it as something good. Once I heard a caregiver tell a terminally ill patient: "Death is part of the lifecycle. It is a beautiful thing to be embraced." This will not do. Death is not part of the lifecycle God originally created. It is the result of the fall. It is by the trespass of one man, Adam, that death reigned through that man (Rom. 5:17). God made this clear to Adam after he and Eve rebelled against God in the Garden of Eden. He said that Adam would return to the ground from which he was taken because "dust you are and to dust you will return" (Gen. 3:19).

Of course, there was an act of grace in all of this. According to Genesis 3:22, God said, "The man . . . must not be allowed to reach out his hand and take also from the tree of life and eat, and live forever." Imagine living on and on and on in a body that continues to deteriorate and decay because of arthritis, cancer, heart disease, and every other effect of sin. Who wants to live forever as each birthday brings an increase in pain and a greater loss of vision and hearing? There is some relief in death from physical and emotional suffering. But it is not something beautiful to be embraced.

No wonder the apostle Paul "trash-talks" death in 1 Corinthians 15:54–57. He begins by citing Isaiah 25:8, which says that God "will swallow up death forever." Then he mocks death for losing its victory and its sting. The term *sting* denotes the sting of a venomous scorpion (Rev. 9:10) or the sharp iron goad that was used not only as an instrument to drive cattle but as an instrument of torture or punishment.[1] When Paul says that "the sting of death is sin," he reminds us "that death is not simply the result of decay through normal human processes. Rather, it is the result of the deadly poison, sin itself, which became all the more energized in our lives through acquaintance with the law."[2] In summary, Paul's whole taunt presses home "the powerlessness of death to damage, to intimidate, or to dismay."[3] Finally, Paul reminds us that this victory is "through our Lord Jesus Christ." It is tied to Jesus's death and resurrection.

Jesus himself made it clear that the resurrection results in the defeat of death. He made this point while arguing with a group of religious leaders who did not believe in the resurrection (Luke 20:27). But Jesus clearly stated that children of the resurrection "no longer die" (v. 36). They do not become angels, but they become like angels in that they possess immortality.

As I write this, I mourn for my cousin and his children. Their wife and mother lost her life a few days ago due to complications caused by Huntington's disease. She was in her mid-forties. Her death reminds me that we cannot escape physical death in our present life. Thankfully, she has victory through our Lord Jesus Christ as one of his children through faith. She will rise again because death is a defeated enemy. This truly is good news!

22

To Give Us a Reason to Endanger Our Lives

> And as for us, why do we endanger ourselves every hour? I face death every day—yes, just as surely as I boast about you in Christ Jesus our Lord.
>
> 1 Corinthians 15:30–31

Throughout 1 Corinthians 15, the apostle Paul uses a variety of arguments to defend the validity of the resurrection. One of these arguments is human behavior. The resurrection has to be true, he argues, for only the resurrection can account for some of the practices he observes in himself and others. One of these practices was endangering his life every day.

But before discussing this particular practice, Paul argues for the validity of the resurrection based on the practice of baptism for the dead. In 1 Corinthians 15:29, he writes: "Now if there is no resurrection, what will those do who are baptized for the dead? If the dead are not raised at all, why are people baptized for them?" Obviously, this seems troubling. This practice seems at odds with receiving the gospel through faith in Jesus Christ—a teaching Paul emphasizes at the beginning of his discussion (1 Cor. 15:2) and which the New Testament emphasizes again and again. But there is no hint here that Paul is condoning baptism for the dead. He simply cites a theologically absurd practice for the sake of argument. It resembles the kind of argument that says, "If God does not exist, then why do atheists pray to him when they face a crisis?" Or, "If God does not exist, then why do thousands of people in baseball stadiums sing 'God Bless America'?" Such arguments do not endorse atheists who pray, or people who have no time for God yet pray for his blessing, any more than Paul endorses those who practice baptism for the dead. This kind of an argument simply reasons that the only way to account for such rituals is the truth of a major claim within Christianity.

In 1 Corinthians 15:30–31, Paul reasons from a type of human behavior he and other Christians display. It is the practice of constantly putting one's life in harm's way. That is the point of the "every hour" and "every day" language. His point is: "On a daily basis I face the reality of death."[1]

Paul was not speaking abstractly. In verse 32, he refers to fighting "wild beasts" in Ephesus. This is certainly a metaphor and not a literal reference to fighting lions in the arena. Likely, it refers to those people who opposed him while he was staying at Ephesus (16:9). In another letter to the church in ancient Corinth, he writes:

> I have worked much harder, been in prison more frequently, been flogged more severely, and been exposed to death again and again. Five times I received from the Jews the forty lashes minus one. Three times I was beaten with rods, once I was pelted with stones, three times I was shipwrecked, I spent a night and a day in the open sea, I have been constantly on the move. I have been in danger from rivers, in danger from bandits, in danger from my fellow Jews, in danger from Gentiles; in danger in the city, in danger in the country, in danger at sea; and in danger from false believers. (2 Cor. 11:23–26)[2]

For Paul, then, there is no possible explanation for Christians putting their lives at constant risk and in such danger except for the resurrection of Jesus Christ. The cost is high. But the resurrection gives us a reason to endanger our lives for the gospel today, tomorrow, and every day after that.

To Deliver Us
from Self-Indulgence

> If I fought wild beasts in Ephesus with no more than human hopes, what have I gained? If the dead are not raised, "Let us eat and drink, for tomorrow we die."
>
> 1 Corinthians 15:32

If the resurrection did not happen, then we might as well pursue a life of self-indulgence, because nothing we have accomplished will last. This is Paul's argument in 1 Corinthians 15:32.

As noted previously, Paul's reference to fighting wild beasts is certainly a metaphor and not a literal reference to fighting lions in the arena. This is the case for two reasons. First, Paul's Roman citizenship would have excluded him from a literal fight in the arena.[1] Second, it seems unlikely that Paul would have survived such an ordeal. Lions would have certainly torn him to pieces. Therefore, Paul must be using this strong language to refer to those people who opposed him while he was staying at Ephesus (16:9). They must have put his life in danger even as they opposed his teaching.

But if there is no resurrection, Paul has engaged in this conflict at a merely human level, as one man fighting against other people. If this is the case, then what has he gained? What has his service to the gospel of Jesus Christ accomplished? The answer is nothing—now and in the life to come.

The alternative, if the dead are not raised, is to pursue a life of self-indulgence. That is the idea behind the expression "let us eat and drink, for tomorrow we die" at the end of verse 32. It is a quotation of Isaiah 22:13, the attitude of the residents of Jerusalem who faced the Assyrian army's siege by partying rather than getting right with God. Such behavior deserves a rebuke. But Paul says, "If the dead are not raised, then you might as well party."

The expression "let us eat and drink, for tomorrow we die" also had relevance to the culture in which Paul and his readers lived. This kind of language was used in Paul's day to describe the Epicureans. It was, perhaps, a bit of an overstatement since the Epicureans did not pursue sheer gluttony and drunkenness as much as they pursued the finer things in life—fine dining, music, theater, and treasured friendships. "Yet ultimately, all of this was self-centered," observes Craig Blomberg, "since they did not look to continuing any pleasures beyond the grave. Self-interest may even lead to humanitarian and altruistic concerns, but ultimately it produces nothing permanently satisfying if this life is all that exists."[2]

But the resurrection of Jesus Christ, and its guarantee of our future resurrection, delivers us from this self-indulgence. It gives us something to live for beyond our own purposes and plans. God has wired us to live for something larger than our own small stories. The writer of Ecclesiastes refers to this when he says that God has "set eternity in the human heart" (Eccles. 3:11). We have a sense that our work and even our lives possess eternal significance, even though we cannot figure it all out. Here the resurrection changes our perspective. It points to and makes possible a better life—something beyond this one, a life more incredible than we can ever imagine. "Recognizing that a far better life awaits us, we can risk our lives or well-being for the gospel"[3] rather than simply living for ourselves.

To Give Us Heavenly, Imperishable Bodies

> So will it be with the resurrection of the dead. The body that is sown is perishable, it is raised imperishable; it is sown in dishonor, it is raised in glory; it is sown in weakness, it is raised in power; it is sown a natural body, it is raised a spiritual body. If there is a natural body, there is also a spiritual body. So it is written: "The first man Adam became a living being"; the last Adam, a life-giving spirit. The spiritual did not come first, but the natural, and after that the spiritual. The first man was of the dust of the earth, the second man is of heaven. As was the earthly man, so are those who are of the earth; and as is the heavenly man, so also are those who are of heaven.
>
> 1 Corinthians 15:42–48

The Clark's Nutcracker is an amazing bird. According to a BBC documentary on Yellowstone National Park, a single bird buries about thirty thousand nuts, or seeds, from the whitebark pine tree every autumn. When winter comes, the bird remembers the location of about 70 percent of the buried seeds. The seeds that remain buried germinate the next spring and grow into whitebark pine trees. Something no less amazing happens to the bodies of Jesus's followers after they die. In fact, the apostle Paul uses the image of planting a seed to establish God's power to bring one living thing through death and into a different mode of existence. He does this to argue against the notion that there is no resurrection.

The apostle Paul sets up this argument by showing how it is not hard to imagine a different kind of bodily existence—that is, life in a resurrected body—because God has created different kinds of bodies. There are different kinds of flesh: humans, animals, birds, and fish (1 Cor. 15:39). Also, there are different kinds of heavenly bodies: sun, moon, stars—and even the stars differ from each other (vv. 40–42). At this point, Paul introduces the analogy of planting a seed. When you plant a seed in the ground, it dies but then comes to life as a stalk of wheat or corn.

We should not be surprised, then, that a different kind of human body can come into existence from our body that dies. The key contrast is between a "natural body" and a "spiritual body." The natural body is what we have now; the spiritual body is what we will have when we are resurrected from death. What, then, is the difference? The terms *natural* and *spiritual* are the same two adjectives Paul used in 1 Corinthians 2:14 to describe the differences between nonbelievers and believers. These terms do not describe the type of material or "stuff" from which the body is made; rather, the natural body is the one that belongs to the life of the present age—the body in the realm of sin, and the spiritual body is the one that will belong to the life of the future age—the age or realm of the Spirit of God.[1] Again, the point is that just as God created a body for the human realm, so he also created a body for the realm of the Spirit.[2]

Now this progression from having natural bodies to spiritual bodies is reasonable because this has already happened in human history. The first human being, Adam, had a natural body. His origin was the dust of the earth. The "last Adam," Jesus Christ, has a spiritual body. His origin is heaven.

Our resurrected bodies, then, will be bodies that have been created for the realm of the Spirit—just like the resurrected body of Jesus. These bodies will be imperishable, meaning that they will never decay! There will be a glory and power to these bodies that will enable us to live life on God's restored earth. Beyond the descriptions Paul gives in this passage, it seems likely that our resurrection bodies will be able to eat like Jesus did in his resurrected state (Luke 24:41–43) and to go through barriers such as doors (John 20:26–27). Even though resurrected people will not marry (Matt. 22:30; Luke 20:35), it is certainly not because our bodies will be less wired for intimacy. Likely, they will be able to experience intimacy with others that goes far beyond the most intimate of human relationships our present bodies are capable of experiencing.[3] We have an amazing life to look forward to in these spiritual bodies because Christ has been raised!

Risen

To Clothe Us with His Image

And just as we have borne the image of the earthly man, so shall we
bear the image of the heavenly man.

1 Corinthians 15:49

I usually appear well dressed because my wife and daughters pay
attention to the clothes I wear. But the clothes I wear now do not
compare to what I will wear when I am resurrected. The most wonderful aspect of life in our resurrected bodies is that they allow us to
bear the image of the man from heaven—the resurrected Christ. The
term *bear* is often used in reference to wearing clothes (Matt. 11:8;
John 19:5; James 2:3). So instead of wearing the image of the earthly
man, Adam, we shall wear the image of Christ. To understand the
significance of this, we must briefly explore a rich, profound theme
in Scripture.

Genesis 1:26–27 informs us that God created man in his image.
Often, Bible readers understand creation in the image of God to mean
that we resemble our Creator; we can reason, love, create, discern,
and so on. This, of course, is true, because Genesis 1:26 also says that
God created us in his likeness. But the original readers would have
understood creation in the image of God to mean something more.
In the Old Testament, the term *image* refers to a statue. Ancient
kings would often set up statues in remote parts of their empires
to represent themselves (Dan. 3:1–15). Because ancient kings often
considered themselves as gods, these statues could be referred to as
"images of god." They provided visible representation of a king who
was otherwise invisible to people living miles away from the palace.
God's Spirit directed the writer of Genesis to use the language of
"image of God" to describe the relationship between God and the
people he created. As "images of God," God's people are his representatives. The fact that they were also created in his likeness means
that they are "representational representatives." That is, they resemble
the God they represent.

After the fall of Adam and Eve into sin, human begins are still considered to be created in the image of God (Gen. 9:6). However, sin has marred the ability of human beings to function as God's images or representatives. Rather than showcasing God's glory, fallen human beings have exchanged it for false worship, impurity, and lies (Rom. 1:21–25).

Into this desperate situation, God sent his Son, Jesus. Colossians 1:15 calls Jesus "the image of the invisible God" (also 2 Cor. 4:4). Amazing! Jesus is the one who perfectly represented God during his life here on earth, glorifying God by putting God's love, power, wisdom, mercy, compassion, and justice on display.

The story gets even more wonderful, though. God's Spirit is currently at work in the lives of Christ's followers, transforming them to be like him (2 Cor. 3:18). It is all part of God's plan. According to Romans 8:29, God's plan is for his children to be conformed to the image of his Son, Jesus![1] This goal will be realized when we are raised to life in spiritual, imperishable bodies like the body of the man from heaven—the resurrected Christ. Then, as we live life in the new earth in these resurrected bodies, we will perfectly represent God by putting his character qualities on display.

I find this encouraging when I get discouraged with my pitiful attempts to represent God in my present condition. I want people to see the beauty of Jesus in me, but I am far too selfish, fearful, and prideful to represent him perfectly. But one day I will represent him perfectly when I am better dressed. One day I will wear the very image of the heavenly man, Jesus Christ, the one who *is* the image of God!

To Give Us Immortality

For the perishable must clothe itself with the imperishable, and the mortal with immortality.

1 Corinthians 15:53

Immortality is a key theme in Stephenie Meyer's *Twilight*, a vampire-romance novel popular among young adults. In the novel, seventeen year-old Bella falls in love with a fellow high school student, Edward, who turns out to be a one-hundred-plus-year-old vampire. When Bella wants Edward to turn her into a vampire, he refuses, knowing how distressing it would be to live forever in such a condition—in what he describes as an "eternity of night."[1] This fictional account captures an important truth: we have a longing to live forever, yet we would not want to live forever in our current state of decay and bondage to sin.

The wonder of the resurrection is that we will live forever in bodies that are not subject to the ravages and decay of sin! When the kingdom of God fully arrives, the bodies of believers in Jesus Christ will be changed. Some believers will be alive at the second coming of Jesus Christ. The dead in Christ will be raised (1 Cor. 15:52). Both will have their bodies "changed from their present state to the one required for God's future."[2] To understand the two parallel statements in 1 Corinthians 15:53 about receiving immortality, we must notice three details.

First, the verb *clothe* is a word picture that simply refers to putting on or wearing clothes. Resurrection resembles putting on a new set of clothes. The Greek philosophers taught that human beings possessed immortality.[3] But the language in 1 Corinthians 15:53 makes it clear that the resurrection brings immortality. The apostle Paul uses similar imagery in another letter to the church in ancient Corinth. He writes:

For we know that if the earthly tent we live in is destroyed, we have a building from God, an eternal house in heaven, not built by human hands. Meanwhile we groan, longing to be clothed instead with our heavenly dwelling, because when we are clothed, we will not be found naked. For while we are in this tent, we groan and are burdened, because we do not wish to be unclothed but to be clothed instead with our heavenly dwelling, so that what is mortal may be swallowed up by life. (2 Cor. 5:1–4)

Murray J. Harris explains: "As a Cilician 'leatherworker' whose duties would include tentmaking, Paul naturally likened his present body to an earthly tent (cf. vv. 2, 4) that might at any moment be dismantled or destroyed."[4] What Paul looks forward to is the resurrection when he is clothed with a new body. The form of the verb in verse 4 pictures the resurrection as putting a new body on top of the present one. It is a new kind of physical existence.

There is a second key detail in 1 Corinthians 15:53 we must note, even though it does not show up in all English translations. Twice, the apostle Paul uses the term *this* in reference to the perishable, mortal body. The ESV captures this well: "For this perishable body must put on the imperishable, and this mortal body must put on immortality." Paul also uses *this* twice in verse 54—literally "this perishable . . . this mortal." So, it is "this" present body that is clothed with a new kind of physicality. There is "clear continuity of identity (*this body*) even in the midst of radical transformation."[5] Even though a believer's body has decomposed or may have been cremated, it will be raised and clothed with something new!

This brings us to a third key detail. The terms *imperishable* and *immortal* describe the new body with which we will be clothed. Although the terms are basically synonymous, they have slightly different emphases. *Imperishable* emphasizes that the body will not wear out or decay. *Immortal* signifies that the body cannot die.[6] Immortality becomes desirable once we know that our resurrection bodies will never lose their hearing, vision, or mobility. No wonder we celebrate the resurrection of Jesus Christ and look forward to the day when we too will be raised from death to a new phase of eternal life!

Jesus was raised from death . . . **27**

To Overcome the Power of the Law

> The sting of death is sin, and the power of sin is the law. But thanks be to God! He gives us the victory through our Lord Jesus Christ.
>
> 1 Corinthians 15:56–57

Within the apostle Paul's thrilling discussion of how the resurrection brings the defeat of death (1 Cor. 15:44–47), he mentions another reason why Christ was raised from death. He was raised to overcome the power of the law. The law to which Paul is referring is the law of Moses—specifically the legal code found in the Old Testament books of Exodus, Leviticus, Numbers, and Deuteronomy. Paul's reasoning goes like this: death has been defeated and has lost its sting. Death's sting comes from sin. Since the law is what empowers sin, the law is defeated too.

Now why does Paul bring up this matter of the law when it has not factored at all thus far in this great resurrection chapter? The answer is that the relationship of the new-covenant believer to the law of Moses was a huge issue in the early church. So it is not surprising that Paul mentions it here, even though he does not take time to develop it. Here is the story behind Paul's passing comment that "the power of sin is the law."

What we sometimes forget is that the law of Moses was a gracious gift of God to a redeemed community (Exod. 19:5; Deut. 4:8; Ps. 19:7–11). This law was not designed as something to be obeyed in order to receive God's salvation. Remember, God saved the people of Israel by bringing them out of Egypt. He stated this at the beginning of the Ten Commandments (Exod. 20:2; Deut. 5:6).[1] Instead, the law was given through Moses to help this saved, redeemed community live the good life God intended for them to experience (Deut. 4:40; 5:33; 6:2–3; 30:19–20).

Over time, however, people fell into various forms of works-based righteousness in which keeping the law supposedly merited God's grace. It is this kind of approach the apostle Paul reacts to when he makes statements like "the power of sin is the law." Now Paul is not saying that the law of Moses is bad or sinful. In fact, he affirms in Romans 7:12 that the law is "holy, righteous, and good." What happened, then, is that evil used the law as its agent. Paul explains this in Romans 7:7–13. He declares that sin seized the opportunity provided by the commandments (v. 11). We might say that evil used the law like electricity uses water. If you try to douse an electrical fire with water, you might end up dead. The electricity would kill you, not the water, but electricity uses the water as a conductor to travel to your body. Similarly, we might think of the law as a surgeon's scalpel. It is meant for life and healing. But sin takes the scalpel of God's commandments and slashes our throats with it.

Paul's point throughout his letters is that the law plays only one role when it comes to our reception of God's salvation: to point out our sinfulness and point us to Christ (Rom. 3:20; Gal. 3:24). Yes, Christians can continue to learn from the law (2 Tim. 3:16–17). As John Calvin says, it "finds its place among believers in whose hearts the Spirit of God already lives and reigns."[2] But the condemning function of the law of Moses has been overcome. Jesus alone satisfied the righteous requirements of the law to set us free from the law of sin and death (Rom. 8:1–4). We will realize this freedom fully at our resurrection when the law no longer empowers us to sin.

This gives me great relief in my struggle with my own sinful tendencies. While Scripture makes it clear that God's grace does not give me a license to sin (6:1–14), I do not need to worry about the law condemning me when I stand before God at judgment day. I do not need to live in uncertainty about where and how I will spend eternity. The resurrection of Jesus Christ, the one I have trusted for God's salvation, brings victory over the law's power to condemn me.

Jesus was raised from death . . . **28**

To Make Serving
the Lord Worthwhile

> Therefore, my dear brothers and sisters, stand firm. Let nothing move
> you. Always give yourselves fully to the work of the Lord, because you
> know that your labor in the Lord is not in vain.
>
> 1 Corinthians 15:58

As followers of Jesus Christ, we are part of an amazing story with a
glorious ending. But right now, as we await that ending, we live in the
"unlovely middle" of the story. Yes, we are beginning to enjoy the new
life here and now (Rom. 6:4; Col. 3:1–3). But we still face the pain of
life in a broken world. Frankly, we sometimes wonder if the gospel is
making any difference. Crime, injustice, violence, sexual abuse, and
hatred only seem to escalate. Even within the church, Jesus's followers
often behave poorly. We complain, covet, lie, and cheat on our spouses.

When Paul wrote to the Corinthians, he wrote to a church that
struggled with false beliefs and inappropriate behavior. There was
division in the Corinthian church as different groups of people idol-
ized different leaders (1 Cor. 1:10–12; 3:1–4). The church struggled
as well with pride and arrogance (4:6–21; 8:1) to the point that its
members flaunted their spiritual gifts.[1] Inexplicably, believers even
tolerated and took pride in a man who was living incestuously with
his stepmother (5:1–13). Paul also called out the church for lawsuits
(6:1–11), sexual immorality with prostitutes (6:12–20), abuse of their
freedom in Christ (8:9–13), as well as gluttony and drunkenness at
the Lord's Supper (11:17–22). Why belong to a church if that is what
you get? Why preach the good news if people who identify themselves
as Christ-followers fail to respond?

The answer is the resurrection. The term *therefore* in 1 Corinthians
15:58 signals that Paul is drawing an implication from everything he
has said about Christ's resurrection and ours in this chapter. Rather
than giving in to cynicism or despair over the sinful behavior of the
church, Paul urges loyalty to the gospel. He does this in two ways.

First, he calls believers to stand firm and let nothing move them. They must not allow the pathetic lifestyle of certain Christians or skepticism toward the idea of bodily resurrection to leave them unsettled.

Second, on the positive side, Paul calls believers to give themselves fully to the work of the Lord. The verb translated "give yourselves fully" can also be translated as "be always abounding" or "overflow." This is the language of extravagance and excess. Rather than pull back, we are to push forward in our service of the gospel. The reason for this is that our labor in the Lord is not in vain. The expression "in vain" means *empty*. Sometimes we wonder if sharing the gospel, caring for the poor, bearing the burdens of other believers, correcting believers who sin, and speaking the truth in love make any difference. According to Paul, they do! The resurrection is what gives it all significance and meaning and success. Christ's resurrection, as well as ours, gives victory to the cause of Christ. We will see limited success in this age. But the ultimate success of the gospel will come together when we are raised as Christ was raised.

What is striking about 1 Corinthians 15:58 is how it ends where the chapter began. Instead of believing in an empty way by failing to stand in the gospel and to hold firm to it (Paul's fear in vv. 1–2), we can give everything we have to the gospel, confident that it will produce lasting effects in our lives and in the lives of others who stand firm. So keep on sharing Christ's love by volunteering at a soup kitchen or battered women's shelter. Keep on teaching a ladies' Bible study or a Sunday school class for a group of third graders. Keep on praying for the sick. Keep on mentoring a new generation of leaders. Keep on serving as an elder or deacon in your local church. Stand firm in the good news that Jesus Christ died for our sins and rose on the third day.

To Give Us Hope in Hard Times

> We do not want you to be uninformed, brothers and sisters, about
> the troubles we experienced in the province of Asia. We were under
> great pressure, far beyond our ability to endure, so that we despaired
> of life itself. Indeed, we felt we had received the sentence of death.
> But this happened that we might not rely on ourselves but on God,
> who raises the dead. He has delivered us from such a deadly peril,
> and he will deliver us again. On him we have set our hope that he will
> continue to deliver us as you help us by your prayers. Then many will
> give thanks on our behalf for the gracious favor granted us in answer
> to the prayers of many.
>
> 2 Corinthians 1:8–11

Have you ever faced a life-threatening situation as a result of your
commitment to serve Jesus Christ? Few believers in the western hemi-
sphere have faced such a threat. But the apostle Paul did while he was
serving Christ in Asia. Paul's troubles—literally "our affliction" or
"our trial"—were so severe that he expected to die. He was burdened
excessively, far beyond his strength. At the time, Paul felt like he was
under a death sentence from which he could not escape.

We can only speculate as to the nature of this affliction. Perhaps it
was his conflict with the "wild beasts" at Ephesus—those opponents
who put his life in danger while he was teaching there (1 Cor. 15:32;
16:9). Perhaps Paul's affliction was connected specifically to the riot at
Ephesus that Demetrius the silversmith instigated when Paul's preaching hurt his idol-manufacturing business (Acts 19:23–41). Perhaps it
was the thirty-nine lashes he received after being arraigned by local
Jewish leaders (2 Cor. 11:24). Perhaps some kind of physical illness
factored into this.[1]

Whatever the nature of his trial, Paul sees a purpose in it. The
purpose is to teach him to rely on God who raises the dead. Three
times in 2 Corinthians 1:10, Paul speaks about God's deliverance from
trial. The first time he refers to past deliverance. The next two times
he anticipates God's future deliverance. His hope comes from a God

who raises the dead. Now why does Paul describe God this particular way in this particular discussion? Elsewhere in 2 Corinthians, Paul describes God as "our Father" (1:2), the "Father of our Lord Jesus Christ" (1:3; 11:31), "the Father of compassion and the God of all comfort" (1:3), "faithful" (1:18), the one "who always leads us as captives in Christ's triumphal procession" (2:14), the one who said "let light shine out of darkness" (4:6), "living" (6:16), and the one "who comforts the downcast" (7:6). So why in this passage does Paul highlight God's act of raising the dead? This mention of God's people being raised from death—something Paul discussed at length in his previous letter to the Corinthian church (1 Cor. 15:1–58)—served to highlight God's power. Paul's language in 2 Corinthians 1:9 is even bolder than we might realize. Paul refers here to God not only as the one who raised Jesus, but as the one who "raises the dead"—plural! Here, as in 1 Corinthians 15:20–23, he anticipates our future resurrection as the logical consequence of Jesus's resurrection.

It is one thing for God to be compassionate to his children when they face extreme distress. But if he is not powerful enough to intervene and rescue them from these deadly situations, then there is no reason for hope and no reason to pray. God's ability to raise the dead demonstrates his power to rescue his people from life-threatening situations. Interestingly, as Paul wraps up 2 Corinthians, he returns to the theme of God's power and alludes to the resurrection when he says: "He [Christ] was crucified in weakness, yet he lives by God's power. Likewise, we are weak in him, yet by God's power we will live with him in our dealing with you" (13:4).

This changes the way we can deal with trials here and now. Instead of wondering if God is present and powerful enough to help us, we can remember that he is the God who raises the dead—giving us confidence and courage to press on. Knowing that the God who raised Jesus from death will one day raise us to new bodily life gives us "strength for today and bright hope for tomorrow" even when our present circumstances seem overwhelming.[2]

Jesus was raised from death . . . **30**

To Give Us a Greater Purpose in Life

And he died for all, that those who live should no longer live for themselves but for him who died for them and was raised again.

2 Corinthians 5:15

In Greek mythology, Narcissus was a young man who fell in love with his own reflection the first time he saw it while bending down to take a drink from a pond. He kept plunging his arms into the water, trying to clasp the neck he saw there.[1] Unfortunately, some of us adopt this as our approach to life. We become narcissists who are self-absorbed and self-centered. We love ourselves so much that our interests, our needs, our desires, and our concerns completely shape the way we spend our time, money, and talent. Jesus told a parable about a rich man who adopted this approach to life. The first part of the parable describes this man.

The ground of a certain rich man yielded an abundant harvest. He thought to himself, "What shall I do? I have no place to store my crops." Then he said, "This is what I'll do. I will tear down my barns and build bigger ones, and there I will store my surplus grain. And I'll say to myself, 'You have plenty of grain laid up for many years. Take life easy; eat, drink and be merry.'" (Luke 12:16–19)

Notice how the terms *I, my,* or *myself* appear ten times in this man's thoughts and words. And when he finally uses the term *you*, it is in reference to himself!

Jesus's death and resurrection make it possible for us to live for someone greater than ourselves. In 2 Corinthians 5:14, the apostle Paul writes, "For Christ's love compels us, because we are convinced that one died for all, and therefore all died."

There is a dispute as to whom Paul is referring in his three uses of "all" in verses 14–15. If the reference is to believers in Christ, then the

73

statement "therefore all died" in verse 14 refers to a believer's death to sin's penalty and to the self-life.[2] The result is that those who live—that is, these believers in Christ—no longer live for themselves but for the crucified, resurrected Lord! But if the three uses of "all" denote all people in general, the contrast is even more striking. Murray J. Harris explains: "While all persons died, in one sense, when the Man who represented them died, not all were raised to new life when he rose."[3] Only those who are in Christ, through faith in him, live!

Once again, the death and the resurrection of Christ appear as twin elements of the gospel (1 Cor. 15:3–8). We are not called to live for a dead Savior but a living One! This leads Paul to affirm: "Therefore, if anyone is in Christ, the new creation has come: The old has gone, the new is here!" (2 Cor. 5:17). We are living creatures by virtue of our connection to the living Christ. This echoes Paul's teaching in Romans 6:4 that "just as Christ was raised from the dead through the glory of the Father, we too may live a new life."

The way that we live for the One who was crucified and raised for us is spelled out in 2 Corinthians. Paul writes:

> We are therefore Christ's ambassadors, as though God were making his appeal through us. We implore you on Christ's behalf: Be reconciled to God. God made him who had no sin to be sin for us, so that in him we might become the righteousness of God. (2 Cor. 5:20–21)

Living for Christ means that we will live for others by sharing with them the message of reconciliation. What person in your circle of relationships needs to hear this message?

To Let Us Experience God's Mighty Power

> I pray that the eyes of your heart may be enlightened in order that you may know the hope to which he has called you, the riches of his glorious inheritance in his holy people, and his incomparably great power for us who believe. That power is the same as the mighty strength he exerted when he raised Christ from the dead and seated him at his right hand in the heavenly realms.
>
> Ephesians 1:18–20

Where do we find the power to overcome anger, resist greed, offer forgiveness, or pursue sexual purity? The answer, according to one of the apostle Paul's prayers, is found in the resurrection of Jesus Christ. In Ephesians 1:18–20, Paul prays for believers to experience God's "resurrection power" through a personal, intimate relationship with God. Although Paul wrote his letter in Greek, he was steeped in the Hebrew Bible—that is, the Old Testament. When he prayed that believers would "know" God's incomparably great power, his idea of "knowing" came right from the Old Testament.

Throughout the Old Testament, the verb *know* and the noun *knowledge* refer to intimacy and relationship, not simply a cognitive understanding of the facts. This is obvious when the writer of Genesis says that Adam "*knew* Eve his wife, and she conceived" (Gen. 4:1 ESV, emphasis added). This is also apparent when 1 Samuel 2:12 says that Eli's sons were wicked men who did not *know* Yahweh. As priests, these sons certainly understood the facts about God, but they did not have a relationship with him. The prophet Jeremiah proclaims that knowledge of God is more valuable than anything else. According to Jeremiah 9:23–24,

> This is what the LORD says: "Let not the wise boast of their wisdom or the strong boast of their strength or the rich boast of their riches, but let the one who boasts boast about this: that they have the understanding

to know me, that I am the LORD, who exercises kindness, justice and righteousness on earth, for in these I delight," declares the LORD.

In Ephesians 1:18–20, the apostle Paul's prayer reveals that growing in the knowledge of God means growing in the knowledge of God's mighty power. This power is one of three aspects of the mighty salvation God won for believers in Christ:

1. the hope to which God has called them,
2. the rich inheritance that he possesses in them, and
3. the mighty power by which he energizes them.[1]

God exercised this power in two ways. First, he raised Christ from the dead (v. 20). Second, he exalted him at his right hand (v. 20) to be head over everything for the church (vv. 21–23).

This is simply remarkable! The power of God we experience in our lives is the same power by which God raised Jesus Christ from death. Paul piles on words for power to make his point. The power he prays we will know is literally "according to the *power* of the *strength* of his *might* which he worked in Christ, raising him from the dead" (vv. 19–20).[2]

As believers in Jesus Christ, we have resurrection power! Oh, how we need to grow in our experience of it, because the struggles we face in life are not merely human conflicts. They are actually conflicts with evil spiritual forces (6:12). Yes, there are dark spiritual powers at work behind the problems Paul discusses in Ephesians—anger, stealing, bitterness, slander, sexual immorality, greed, deception, and so on. The way to combat these forces is to stand in God's mighty power (v. 10)—that is, resurrection power. In Ephesians 6, Paul uses a memory device—the armor of a Roman soldier—to help the Ephesian believers remember the resources he has already discussed in his letter (vv. 13–17). These include truth, righteousness, the gospel of peace, faith, salvation, and the Word of God. All of these pieces of armor must be "put on" with prayer (v. 18).

In our struggle with everything that sets itself against the knowledge of God, we have some incredible resources. When we make use of these resources, we will experience the mighty power with which God raised Christ from death!

Risen

To Display God's Amazing Grace

> And God raised us up with Christ and seated us with him in the heavenly realms in Christ Jesus, in order that in the coming ages he might show the incomparable riches of his grace, expressed in his kindness to us in Christ Jesus.
>
> Ephesians 2:6–7

God put his amazing grace and kindness on display through the resurrection of Jesus Christ. We need to hear this because of the reality of God's wrath. Yes, the Bible presents God as an "angry God" when it comes to sin. Ephesians 2:3 says: "All of us also lived among them [the disobedient] at one time, gratifying the cravings of our flesh and following its desires and thoughts. Like the rest, we were by nature deserving of wrath."

Unfortunately, God's anger makes people angry. Writers in our late modern age like Richard Dawkins and Christopher Hitchens try to use God's wrath against him, portraying him as cruel, vindictive, and barbaric.[1] But as theologian Miroslav Volf observes, "in a world of violence it would not be worthy of God *not to wield* the sword; if God were *not angry* at injustice and deception and *did not* make the final end to violence God would not be worthy of our worship."[2]

Thankfully, the God of wrath is also the God of grace. In his grace and mercy, God found a way to satisfy justice and his righteous outrage against evil. When Jesus was crucified, he absorbed the wrath of God and turned it aside for those who believe in him (Rom. 3:21–26). Ephesians 2:4–5 describes it like this: "But because of his great love for us, God, who is rich in mercy, made us alive with Christ even when we were dead in transgressions—it is by grace you have been saved." So, although anger is part of God's character, his love, grace, and mercy overcome his wrath without diminishing it.

This is precisely what God emphasizes when he passes in front of Moses and proclaims:

The LORD, the LORD, the compassionate and gracious God, slow to anger, abounding in love and faithfulness, maintaining love to thousands, and forgiving wickedness, rebellion and sin. Yet he does not leave the guilty unpunished; he punishes the children and their children for the sin of the parents to the third and fourth generation. (Exod. 34:6–7)

Some Bible readers have missed the point of this. This text does not teach that God punishes children for the sins their ancestors committed. God clearly dismisses such an idea in Ezekiel 18. Rather, it points out that God "visits" sin as it gets passed down from generation to generation. Notice the contrast in numbers. God shows wrath to the third and fourth generations of the guilty. By contrast, he shows his love to thousands. Even the numbers emphasize how God's love and grace and mercy can overcome his wrath!

By the way, grace and mercy are two sides of the same coin. Grace is God giving me what I don't deserve. Mercy is God not giving me what I do deserve.

Now God's mercy and grace do not stop with the cross of Christ. They are also expressed through Christ's resurrection. Ephesians 2:6–7 makes it clear God has raised us with Christ and has seated us in the heavenly realms so that we can experience future grace. No longer are we under the authority of earthly, evil powers. The apostle Paul is so confident of our future that he writes as if it has already taken place. Remember this the next time you are overcome by feelings of guilt and wonder how God can ever accept you. Remember this when you are feeling lonely or depressed or hopeless. Thanks to the resurrection of Jesus Christ, God has raised and exalted us to display his magnificent, extravagant grace for all eternity!

To Bring Victory
into Our Intimacy with Him

> I want to know Christ—yes, to know the power of his resurrection and participation in his sufferings, becoming like him in his death, and so, somehow, attaining to the resurrection from the dead.
>
> Philippians 3:10–11

What is your greatest quest or obsession in life? For one young lady I know, it is becoming a pediatric oncologist. For a middle-aged man I talked to recently, the quest is the growth of his business into one that does one hundred million dollars of business annually. The NFL player I saw the other day at a fast-food restaurant near my house is on a quest to win a Super Bowl. These are lofty pursuits. But they are nothing compared to the apostle Paul's quest and obsession.

For the apostle Paul, knowing Christ became what I like to refer to as his "magnificent obsession." He counts his remarkable Jewish heritage as loss, and even as "dung" when compared to the surpassing worth of knowing Jesus Christ (Phil. 3:7–8). In Philippians 3:10–11, Paul describes the two dimensions in which he wants to know Christ. These dimensions relate to the two aspects of the gospel: the death and resurrection of Jesus Christ. Notice how Paul repeats these elements in reverse order for emphasis:

A. The power of his resurrection
   B. The participation in his sufferings
   B. Becoming like him in his death
A. Attaining to the resurrection from the dead

So, Paul's longing is to know Christ, experiencing the power of Christ's resurrection even as he shares in Christ's suffering in the daily events of life. Paul is not some kind of masochist, one who derives pleasure from pain or mistreatment. But he understands that both the suffering and the resurrection of Jesus give shape to the way we experience the Christian life. Above all, Paul wants to face his present sufferings with resurrection power. Notice how he describes both aspects.

First, on the side of suffering, Paul wants his life to be conformed to, or shaped by, the death of Christ. This takes Paul, and all of us who want to know Christ, back to the humility and obedience Christ displayed in submitting to crucifixion. Living a cross-shaped life resembles a relationship with someone who is battling cancer; if we truly want to experience a relationship with this person, we may shave our heads, follow the same diet, visit the doctor together, and weep together—even though we will not experience exactly what the cancer-stricken person is facing. So it is in our relationship with Christ. We will subject ourselves to humility, ridicule, discrimination, loneliness, and other types of sacrifice—even though we will not experience the same level of suffering that Christ did.

Second, as we are conformed to Christ's death, we handle it with resurrection power and look forward to our own resurrection. Yes, the power of Christ's resurrection is what strengthens us to live for him even as we die with him. When Paul uses the term *somehow*, he is not expressing doubt about whether or not he will experience resurrection. The expression "and so, somehow"—literally "if somehow"— in Philippians 3:11 is actually an expression of expectation![1] Paul's uncertainty is not *if* he will experience resurrection, but *how* he will experience resurrection. Will he be alive at Christ's return and experience bodily transformation? Or will he be resurrected from death?

Knowing the power of Christ's resurrection must accompany sharing in his death. If we simply know suffering without resurrection, we become gloomy, negative, and joyless. If we focus on resurrection without suffering, we become "prosperity gospel" types who will be disillusioned when we suffer. Knowing Christ truly and fully means knowing the power of his resurrection as well as knowing what it means to participate in his suffering and model the way he handled his death. This brings victory into our intimacy with him.

Jesus was raised from death . . .

34

To Make Us Full in Him

> For in Christ all the fullness of the Deity lives in bodily form, and in Christ you have been brought to fullness. He is the head over every power and authority. In him you were also circumcised with a circumcision not performed by human hands. Your whole self ruled by the flesh was put off when you were circumcised by Christ, having been buried with him in baptism, in which you were also raised with him through your faith in the working of God, who raised him from the dead.
>
> Colossians 2:9–12

An old song by John Denver, "I Want To Live," captures what most people, including me, want to get out of life; it expresses the desire to grow, see, know, share, be, and live. What we want is a rich texture to our life. We crave experiences and knowledge. We want our lives to make a difference. We want to live life to its fullest. Unfortunately, we sometimes look for fullness in all the wrong places. True fullness is tied to the resurrection of Jesus Christ.

In Colossians 2, the apostle Paul calls on Christians to be faithful to Christ Jesus as Lord (vv. 6–7) and not let anyone take them "captive through hollow and deceptive philosophy, which depends on human tradition and the elementary spiritual forces of this world rather than on Christ" (v. 8). The reason, according to verses 9–12, is that true "fullness" is available only through the resurrection of Jesus Christ.

The argument goes something like this: Christians must not pursue a philosophy of life that diminishes Christ by mixing in Jewish rituals and pagan magical practices.[1] The reason is that (1) the "fullness" of God is found only in Christ, and (2) followers of Christ have already received this fullness in Christ—the one who rules over all the spiritual powers with which many in the ancient city of Colossae were infatuated.[2]

So how do followers of Christ receive this fullness? It is by being circumcised with the circumcision done by Christ. Circumcision here is a metaphor for spiritual heart surgery, as it is in Deuteronomy 10:16 and Jeremiah 4:4. This spiritual heart surgery happened not through the physical act of circumcision ("done by the hands of men") but with a circumcision done by Christ. This is certainly a metaphor for the death of Christ. But the argument is not finished. In this spiritual heart surgery, followers of Christ participate in this death and resurrection. They have died with him—as signified by their baptism that pictures Christ's burial—and have been raised with him. This has happened through faith in the power of God who raised Christ from the dead.

So, Jesus's resurrection makes it possible for the fullness of God to take up residence in him and for us, his followers, to receive this fullness. Amazing! But what does the apostle Paul mean by the "fullness of God"? If the false teachers in Colossae used the term *fullness* to refer to supernatural powers that existed between God and his creation, then Paul may be using the term in part to undermine this view.[3] But there is a more foundational reason for using the expression "fullness of God." The Old Testament uses the language of fullness to denote the presence of God.[4] "'Do I not fill heaven and earth?' declares the LORD" (Jer. 23:24). Psalm 72:19 says: "May the whole earth be filled with his glory." Ezekiel 43:5 and 44:4 both describe the glory of the Lord filling the temple.

Christ, then, fulfills the role assigned to the temple in the Old Testament.[5] God in all his divine essence and power has taken up residence in Christ![6] Clinton Arnold says: "Christ is not one among a number of powers at a certain level of the angelic hierarchy. He is at the top. He is supreme."[7] Because of Christ's resurrection, then, we can stop looking for fullness in all the wrong places. We can be confident that we have all the resources we need in the resurrected Christ to live a full, rich, meaningful life.

Jesus was raised from death . . .

35

To Reorient Our Desires

> Since, then, you have been raised with Christ, set your hearts on things above, where Christ is, seated at the right hand of God. Set your minds on things above, not on earthly things.
>
> Colossians 3:1–2

C. S. Lewis warns us about a problem we have with our desires, but the problem is not what we might expect. He argues: "Our Lord finds our desires not too strong, but too weak."[1] It is true that Christ calls us to deny ourselves and take up our crosses in order to follow him (Luke 9:23). But we must not interpret this as a call to suppress our desires. Rather, this is a call to redirect our desires.

In Colossians 3:1–2, the apostle Paul calls us to reorient our desires based on our status of being raised with Christ. Even though the resurrection is a future event for believers, it is also a present reality. The truth is, the future has been pulled back into our present experience! Such an idea fits with the teaching of the New Testament, which presents our salvation as "already but not yet." For example, Romans 5:9 touches on both the "already" and the "not yet" when it says, "Since we have now been justified by his blood, how much more shall we be saved from God's wrath through him!"

So what difference should our present experience of Christ's resurrection make in our lives? The apostle Paul explains this in parallel commands. First, he tells us to "set your hearts on things above, where Christ is, seated at the right hand of God" (Col. 3:1). The expression "set your hearts on" is actually the word *seek*. It refers to what we pursue. According to Paul, we are to pursue "the things above." Here Paul seems to use the categories of Jewish rabbis, who referred to two realms—an upper realm and lower realm.[2] When he speaks of "things above," he refers to the heavenly realm, to those things that belong to God. He defines this as the place "where Christ is, seated at the right hand of God." This image does not intend to convey Christ passively sitting on a throne in heaven. Rather, like the portrayal of Abraham

Lincoln seated on a throne in Washington DC's Lincoln Memorial, it is a metaphor for his reign and rule as a powerful king!

Paul uses a different verb when he repeats this command in Colossians 3:2. This time, he instructs believers to "set your minds on"—that is, "focus your thoughts on" or "give your minds to" the things above. When Paul wrote his letter, he actually put the object, "the things above," first in the sentence for emphasis. To make the point even clearer, Paul adds a contrast at the end of the sentence: "not on earthly things." These are things that belong to the old order or old way of life: sexual immorality, impurity, lust, greed, anger, rage, malice, slander, filthy language, and lying (Col. 3:5–9). C. S. Lewis observes:

> We are half-hearted creatures, fooling about with drink and sex and ambition when infinite joy is offered us, like an ignorant child who wants to go on making mud pies in a slum because he cannot imagine what is meant by the offer of a holiday at the sea. We are far too easily pleased.[3]

But the resurrection of Jesus Christ changes everything! The reality of our future resurrection as followers of Christ has been pulled back into the present and has reoriented our desires. My friend and mentor Gerry Breshears says, "As a regenerate person, what I deeply want to do is godly. While doing what is godly may not always be my strongest desire, it is my deepest one (Gal. 5:16–17)."[4] The result, according to Colossians 3:1–2, is that we will attempt to line up our desires with the life Christ's resurrection has made possible. Peter O'Brien summarizes this well: "Since you have shared in Christ's resurrection your aims, ambitions, in fact your whole outlook, are to be centered in him, in that place of highest honor where God has exalted him."[5]

Risen

Jesus was raised from death . . . **36**

To Let Us Appear
with Him in Glory

When Christ, who is your life, appears, then you also will appear with him in glory.

Colossians 3:4

"Men of Galilee," they said, "why do you stand here looking into the sky? This same Jesus, who has been taken from you into heaven, will come back in the same way you have seen him go into heaven."

Acts 1:11

In *The Return of the King*, the final volume of J. R. R. Tolkien's trilogy "The Lord of the Rings," Aragorn returns to Gondor, where he is crowned king. If you have read the book or watched the movie, you remember how Aragorn and his forces defeat the panicked servants of Mordor at the Black Gate. As a result, the Darkness dissipates, allowing Aragorn to assume the throne and bring healing and recovery to his kingdom. The story's resolution alludes to an even more thrilling resolution—the final chapter in God's great story of redemption.

In the Bible's great story, the resurrection of Jesus Christ makes it possible for him to return again to earth. Immediately after Jesus was taken to heaven—an event we call the ascension—a couple of angels explain that he will return "in the same way you have seen him go into heaven" (Acts 1:11). What exactly does this mean? How will Jesus's return to earth resemble his ascension to heaven?

First, just as Jesus ascended to heaven, "he is coming with the clouds" (Rev. 1:7). This detail adds much more than color to the scene. It is an allusion to the event prophesied in Daniel 7:13 where the Messiah, or "Son of Man," comes with the clouds of heaven. According to Daniel's vision, this one receives dominion, glory, and a kingdom that will never be destroyed (v. 14).

Second, just as his ascension was visible, Jesus's coming will be visible. Revelation 1:7 adds that "every eye will see him, even those who pierced him." The contrast is striking. While his ascension to heaven was witnessed by a handful of followers, his return will be witnessed by everyone, including those who rejected him.

Third, Jesus's second coming to earth will be personal. Just as Jesus ascended bodily into heaven, "his appearing will not be a mere spiritual coming to dwell within people's hearts, but will be a *personal* and *bodily* return."[1] As Paul says in 1 Thessalonians 4:16, "the Lord himself will come down from heaven."

But Colossians 3:4 adds a stunning detail to this: at his appearance "you also will appear with him in glory." Paul elsewhere describes our appearing with Christ like this:

> For the Lord himself will come down from heaven, with a loud command, with the voice of the archangel and with the trumpet call of God, and the dead in Christ will rise first. After that, we who are still alive and are left will be caught up together with them in the clouds to meet the Lord in the air. And so we will be with the Lord forever. Therefore encourage one another with these words. (1 Thess. 4:16–18)

We cannot get so caught up in trying to figure out all the details or timing of the events associated with the return of Christ that we miss its significance. The fact that the resurrected Christ will one day be fully revealed is our cause for encouragement when we face discouraging, hopeless patches of life. To use another line from Tolkien's *The Return of the King*, "everything sad is going to come untrue."[2] Think about that. Anxiety, depression, fear, persecution, suffering, and decay will all come untrue when Christ returns. The apostle John says as much when he writes: "Dear friends, now we are children of God, and what we will be has not yet been made known. But we know that when Christ appears, we shall be like him, for we shall see him as he is" (1 John 3:2). We long for Christ's appearing (2 Tim. 4:8) and wait for it as our blessed hope (Titus 2:13)—a hope made possible because Christ has been raised from death!

To Enable Us to Kill
Our Old Way of Life

> Put to death, therefore, whatever belongs to your earthly nature: sexual immorality, impurity, lust, evil desires and greed, which is idolatry. Because of these, the wrath of God is coming. You used to walk in these ways, in the life you once lived. But now you must also rid yourselves of all such things as these: anger, rage, malice, slander, and filthy language from your lips. Do not lie to each other, since you have taken off your old self with its practices and have put on the new self, which is being renewed in knowledge in the image of its Creator.
>
> Colossians 3:5–10

A few years ago, we built a house on a small hill overlooking a beautiful valley. We planted grass seed for a new lawn. When the new lawn began to grow, we had to work hard at killing the weeds that kept sprouting up. I spent hours spraying weed killer on dandelions, thistles, quack grass, and chickweed. This resembles what we have to do as followers of Christ. Even though God gives us new birth when we turn to Christ through faith (1 Pet. 1:3–5), we have to be diligent about putting to death the actions of the old life.

Killing the actions of the old life, though, is not something we do in our own power. Rather, it flows out of the apostle Paul's teaching about our union with the resurrected Christ. Putting to death the actions of the old life is possible and necessary precisely because we have been raised with Christ and will one day be raised to appear with him in glory (Col. 3:1–4).

So exactly what actions do we kill since they are part of the old way of life and do not belong to our resurrection life? Paul provides two lists in Colossians 3:5–10. The first list moves from outward acts of sin to the inner cravings of the heart,[1] and some of the terms overlap. The expression "sexual immorality" refers to a wide variety of sexual behaviors outside the boundary of marriage. Similarly, "impurity" refers to immoral sexual conduct. "Lust" translates a term Paul uses to refer to shameful passion that leads to sexual excesses. So the way we handle our sexuality must not contradict the new way of life to which we have been raised in Christ.

As Paul's first list continues, he moves to the inner thoughts or emotions that lead to outward behavior. The phrase "evil desires" refers to desires or longings. While the term *desire* itself is neutral and can refer to positive desires,[2] it refers here to desires that lead to immoral, impure sexual acts. The final term in the list is "greed." Here, Paul makes a fascinating observation: greed is essentially idolatry. When we hear the word *idolatry* we are likely to think of people bowing down before statues or figurines. But an idol is simply a substitute for God.[3] An idol is anything to which we look for the security, significance, and salvation that only God can provide. Idols may even be good things such as a career, physical appearance, academic achievements, relationships, and material wealth. But when we make "God things" out of these "good things," we end up in sexual immorality, pride, fear, depression, or greed.

In Paul's second list, he moves from inward sins to outward sins of speech. "Anger" and "rage" likely overlap to cover everything from a more settled feeling of hatred to outbursts of anger. "Malice" refers to intent to harm. "Slander" refers to evil speech against God or humans, and "filthy language" covers any kind of obscene or abusive speech.

The bottom line is that we are not to live like we used to live, because we are no longer the earthly people we used to be. We are to kill the old ways of life, which spring up like weeds. We can and must do this because we have been raised with Christ—the one who was raised through the power of God from death.

Jesus was raised from death . . . **38**

To Rescue Us from Coming Wrath

> To wait for his Son from heaven, whom he raised from the dead—Jesus, who rescues us from the coming wrath.
>
> 1 Thessalonians 1:10

Perhaps the most terrifying sentence that children hear from their mothers when they have been disobedient is: "Wait until your father gets home!" No child likes to face the wrath of their father for their wrongdoing. Sometimes, believers feel like this about their heavenly Father. They fear that God is angry with them. But this fear is unfounded because of Jesus's resurrection. If God had not raised Jesus from the dead, then believers would have no one to rescue them from the coming wrath. Once again, the resurrection changes everything! Think for a moment about how it relates to the wrath of God.

The coming wrath is God's wrath against sinful people. In the present, God pours out his wrath against sinners by giving them to their sinful desires (Rom. 1:24–32). The result is self-destruction and misery. But a future day is coming when God will pour out his wrath on the disobedient in an even more severe way (Eph. 5:5–6; Col. 3:5–6). In 2 Thessalonians 1:7–9, the apostle Paul writes:

> This will happen when the Lord Jesus is revealed from heaven in blazing fire with his powerful angels. He will punish those who do not know God and do not obey the gospel of our Lord Jesus. They will be punished with everlasting destruction and shut out from the presence of the Lord and from the glory of his might.

Even Jesus speaks frequently and graphically about God's outpouring of wrath in the future judgment. For example, Jesus said to people who refused to turn to him for salvation: "But I tell you that it will be more bearable for Sodom on the day of judgment than for you" (Matt. 11:24). Sodom was one of two cities God destroyed with burning sulfur for its wickedness in the time of Abraham (Gen. 19:24–25). Jesus warned people about hell (Matt. 5:22, 29–30; 10:28;

18:9; 23:15, 33) and also talked about God assigning rebels to "eternal fire" and "eternal punishment" (25:41, 46).

Many struggle with the idea of a loving God who expresses wrath. But wrath is not at odds with God's love, nor is it a characteristic that portrays God in a negative way. I. Howard Marshall explains it well:

> When Paul uses the word [wrath] it generally means not an emotion felt by God but the unpleasant measures which are taken against sinners. There is no sense in which God feels angry like a human person whose pride has been hurt and who bursts out with a fit of temper and passion. Rather, if God is holy, pure and righteous, then his wrath represents a just reaction to the wickedness of those who spoil and destroy the perfect society which it was his intention to create. God's wrath is always directed against evil and is not arbitrary and unprincipled.[1]

Even though the resurrection of Christ testifies to the reality of God's judgment on the world (Acts 17:31), Christ's followers can be encouraged by his return. Paul argues this later in his letter, in 1 Thessalonians 4:13–5:11. In the course of this argument, he writes: "For God did not appoint us to suffer wrath but to receive salvation through our Lord Jesus Christ" (5:9). This is possible because he both "died for us" (v. 10) and was "raised from the dead" (1:10).

So, if you are a believer in Jesus Christ, be encouraged that Jesus, for whose return you wait, is not coming to pour out wrath upon you. Rather, because he "has already suffered the end-time wrath for his people at the cross,"[2] the risen Christ will return to rescue us from that wrath and to enjoy the Lord's presence forever (1 Thess. 4:17).

Jesus was raised from death . . . **39**

To Serve as Our Eternal Shepherd

> The God of peace, who through the blood of the eternal covenant brought back from the dead our Lord Jesus, that great Shepherd of the sheep.
>
> Hebrews 13:20

> For the Lamb at the center of the throne will be their shepherd;
> "he will lead them to springs of living water."
> "And God will wipe away every tear from their eyes."
>
> Revelation 7:17

The shepherd image is one of the most meaningful images in the Bible when it comes to describing God's care and protection of his people.[1] The first time the Bible describes God as shepherd is in Genesis 48:15 when Jacob refers to "the God before whom my fathers Abraham and Isaac walked faithfully" as "the God who has been my shepherd all my life to this day." The most well-known use of the image in the Old Testament is in Psalm 23 where the writer, David, declares: "The LORD is my shepherd, I lack nothing" (v. 1). Because God is his shepherd, David ends Psalm 23 by affirming:

> Surely, goodness and loyal love will pursue me
> all the days of my life.
> And I will live in the house of the LORD forever.[2]

In the New Testament, Jesus applies the shepherd image to himself. Likening the religious leaders of his day to hired hands, Jesus says:

> I am the good shepherd. The good shepherd lays down his life for the sheep. The hired hand is not the shepherd and does not own the sheep. So when he sees the wolf coming, he abandons the sheep and runs away. Then the wolf attacks the flock and scatters it. The man runs away because he is a hired hand and cares nothing for the sheep. I am the good shepherd; I know my sheep and my sheep know me. (John 10:11–14)

But Jesus knew that he, the good shepherd, would be killed. According to Matthew 26:31, Jesus told his followers: "This very night you will all fall away on account of me, for it is written: 'I will strike the shepherd, and the sheep of the flock will be scattered.'"

All is not lost, though, thanks to the resurrection. Hebrews 13:20 makes it clear that "The God of peace . . . through the blood of the eternal covenant brought back from the dead our Lord Jesus, that great Shepherd of the sheep." Jesus lives, then, to serve as "the Shepherd and Overseer of your souls" (1 Pet. 2:25). Even more, Jesus, the Lamb, will serve as our shepherd in our eternal home (Rev. 7:17). As our shepherd, he will remove sorrow and will lead us to springs of living water. In Jesus's day, the Jewish rabbis placed a value on "living water"—water that was flowing from a spring or in a stream—as opposed to water drawn from a well, cistern, or pond.[3] Only the living water "could be used in ritual washings to make pure unclean worshipers."[4] When applied to Jesus, the metaphor points to his role as the one who brings spiritual purity, life, and renewal.

I turn to the shepherding metaphor quite often because I face trials and setbacks and disappointments quite often. During times of difficulty, I often pray the words of an old hymn:

> Savior, like a shepherd lead us,
> Much we need Thy tender care;
> In Thy pleasant pastures feed us,
> For our use Thy folds prepare:
> Blessed Jesus, blessed Jesus,
> Thou has bought us, Thine we are.[5]

Without the resurrection of Jesus Christ, he would not be able to serve as the eternal shepherd. But because he has risen from the dead, he continues to serve as our good shepherd forever!

Jesus was raised from death . . .   **40**

To Give Us New Birth
into a Living Hope

Praise be to the God and Father of our Lord Jesus Christ! In his great mercy he has given us new birth into a living hope through the resurrection of Jesus Christ from the dead.

1 Peter 1:3

Then Paul, knowing that some of them were Sadducees and the others Pharisees, called out in the Sanhedrin, "My brothers, I am a Pharisee, descended from Pharisees. I stand on trial because of the hope of the resurrection of the dead."

Acts 23:6

Brothers and sisters, we do not want you to be uninformed about those who sleep in death, so that you do not grieve like the rest of mankind, who have no hope. For we believe that Jesus died and rose again, and so we believe that God will bring with Jesus those who have fallen asleep in him.

1 Thessalonians 4:13–14

Game six of the 2011 World Series will go down as one of the greatest games in World Series history. Twice, the St. Louis Cardinals were within one strike of losing the game and the World Series to the Texas Rangers. Twice, the Cardinals rallied to tie the game and send it to extra innings—and they won it on a dramatic walk-off home run. Then they won the seventh and final game the following night. A friend of mine, who shelled out several hundred dollars for tickets to attend game six, told me that dozens of fans never saw the dramatic comebacks. They had left the stadium early, thinking that the situation was hopeless.

We may feel the same way about our situation in life. Things appear hopeless. Marriages turn sour. The economy worsens. Our health declines. Our struggles with sin seem to escalate. Hope is gone. But there is a reason for hope, and that reason is the new birth. Jesus makes it clear to Nicodemus, a leading religious leader, that new birth is essential for experiencing life in God's kingdom. Jesus declares, "Very truly I tell you, no one can see the kingdom of God unless they are born again" (John 3:3). The new birth Jesus discusses is the supernatural creation of new life by the Holy Spirit in a person who was spiritually dead (vv. 3–8). Since all of us begin life on earth in a spiritually dead condition (Eph. 2:3), all of us need this new birth (also called *regeneration*).

This need for new birth is so desperate that the prophets talked about it hundreds of years before Jesus came to earth. For example, the prophet Ezekiel recorded God's description of what he would do:

> I will give you a new heart and put a new spirit in you; I will remove from you your heart of stone and give you a heart of flesh. And I will put my Spirit in you and move you to follow my decrees and be careful to keep my laws. (Ezek. 36:26–27)

The need for new birth is so desperate that it can only happen through the work of the Holy Spirit (Ezek. 36:27; John 3:5–8) and through the word of truth—the gospel of Jesus Christ (James 1:18; 1 Pet. 1:18–23). The need for new birth is so desperate that it took the resurrection of Jesus Christ to make it possible. This is the point of 1 Peter 1:3. John Piper explains:

> The new birth is something that happens to us when the Holy Spirit takes our dead hearts and unites us to Christ by faith so that his life becomes our life. . . . The new life we get in the new birth is the life of the historical Jesus. Therefore, if he does not rise from the dead, there is no new life to have.[1]

First Peter 1:3 says that the outcome of the new birth is a "living hope." This was important to the people to whom Peter wrote because they were facing suffering. With the prospect of more pain and suffering ahead of them, they needed the hope of a better future—even hope that death would not be an end for them, but a beginning. The apostle Paul felt the same way. He faced suffering, including a trial before religious authorities, because of his hope in the resurrection of the dead (Acts 23:6). He even used future hope to instruct believers about how to grieve when they lost loved ones. Believers in Christ grieve when loved ones or friends die. But according to Paul, we must not "grieve like the rest of mankind, who have no hope" (1 Thess. 4:13). Our grief is shaped by the gospel. "We believe that Jesus died and rose again, and so we believe that God will bring with Jesus those who have fallen asleep in him" (v. 14). Thank God for the resurrection of Christ that gives us new birth into this living hope!

41 *Jesus was raised from death . . .*
To Glorify the Lamb of God

For you know that it was not with perishable things such as silver or gold that you were redeemed from the empty way of life handed down to you from your ancestors, but with the precious blood of Christ, a lamb without blemish or defect. He was chosen before the creation of the world, but was revealed in these last times for your sake. Through him you believe in God, who raised him from the dead and glorified him, and so your faith and hope are in God.

1 Peter 1:18–21

The God of Abraham, Isaac and Jacob, the God of our fathers, has glorified his servant Jesus. You handed him over to be killed, and you disowned him before Pilate, though he had decided to let him go. You disowned the Holy and Righteous One and asked that a murderer be released to you. You killed the author of life, but God raised him from the dead. We are witnesses of this.

Peter (Acts 3:13–15)

Christopher Parkening, America's preeminent classical guitarist, dealt his a career a deathblow in the late 1970s when he decided to retire and move to Montana. He put his guitar down and spent his days riding horses and fly fishing. When he decided to resume his career five years later, his agent warned him that he might not be able to get it back. The turning point came when Parkening premiered a "Bach suite"—a selection of music from the cantatas of Johann Sebastian Bach—with the Cincinnati Pops. This concert showed Parkening's glory as a classical guitarist. It displayed the glory that was hidden when he set aside his career.[1] In a similar yet more stunning way, an event in Jesus's life put on display the glory that was hidden when Jesus took on human flesh and gave his life as a sacrifice for sin. This event, of course, was the resurrection.

The apostle Peter made this point in a sermon shortly after Jesus ascended to heaven. In that sermon, Peter declared that God "has glorified his servant Jesus" (Acts 3:13) and offered as evidence the fact that "God raised him from the dead" (v. 15). Then, he made the same

96

point several years later in a letter to a group of suffering Christians when he described God as the one "who raised [Christ] from the dead and glorified him" (1 Pet. 1:21).

What Peter does in both his sermon and his letter is pick up language from the opening verse of the great song of the suffering servant in Isaiah 52:

> See, my servant will act wisely;
> he will be raised and lifted up and highly exalted. (v. 13)

Throughout the song of the suffering servant, Isaiah 52:13–53:12, we learn that the servant will suffer for the sins of God's people. His appearance is disfigured (52:14). He is despised and rejected by men (53:3). He is a man of sorrows (v. 3). He is like a lamb led to the slaughter (v. 7). He is cut off from the land of the living (v. 8). He is crushed by God (v. 10). But all this horrible suffering had a point! He became a substitute for his people. Isaiah 53:5 puts it so clearly:

> But he was pierced for our transgressions,
> he was crushed for our iniquities;
> the punishment that brought us peace was on him,
> and by his wounds we are healed.

Yet the very beginning of the servant song—the words to which Peter alludes in his sermon and letter—point to a glorious outcome. The servant will be raised, lifted up, and highly exalted. That last expression, "highly exalted," was translated *glorified* in the Greek Old Testament—the version of the Old Testament Peter would have used. God did not leave his servant and his lamb defeated by death. God raised Jesus to life, establishing that Jesus's death was a victory and a success. Yes, God vindicated his suffering servant. The resurrection showcased the glory and honor of Jesus. It highly exalted him in the eyes of those who might doubt his integrity of power because of his death. This encourages me on days when people ridicule my faith in Jesus Christ and on days when the church I serve seems less than glorious. Whenever I am tempted to wonder if I have given my life to a lost cause, I remember how the resurrection of Jesus Christ put his glory and honor on display. That is why my faith and my hope are in God!

42

Jesus was raised from death . . .

To Show That Death Does Not Stop Us from Living

At the resurrection people will neither marry nor be given in marriage; they will be like the angels in heaven. But about the resurrection of the dead—have you not read what God said to you, "I am the God of Abraham, the God of Isaac, and the God of Jacob"? He is not the God of the dead but of the living.

Jesus (Matthew 22:30–32)

For this very reason, Christ died and returned to life so that he might be the Lord of both the dead and the living.

Romans 14:9

Does God's care for his people stop when they die? Does death separate us from God's love, God's purposes, God's protection, and God's plan? Jesus offers us an answer with overwhelming encouragement in a discussion he has about the resurrection with the Sadducees—a group of wealthy families of priests in Jerusalem. The Sadducees denied the resurrection (Matt. 22:23), believing that both body and soul perished at death.[1] The discussion began when the Sadducees came to Jesus with what we call a trick question. They asked about a widow's marital status at the resurrection. In their story (vv. 24–28), a man dies, leaving his widow childless. So, according to the law of Moses, this man's brother marries her. He, too, dies, leaving her childless. As a result, a second brother marries her. He, too, dies, leaving her childless. This happens with five more brothers—seven in all! Eventually, the woman dies. The trick question asked by the Sadducees is: "Now then, at the resurrection, whose wife will she be of the seven, since all of them were married to her?" (v. 28).

Jesus's reply is blunt: "You are in error because you do not know the Scriptures or the power of God" (v. 29). Then he makes two key points. The first is a direct response to their foolish question. He says: "At the resurrection people will neither marry nor be given in marriage; they will be like the angels in heaven" (v. 30). This answer is all the more interesting since the Sadducees denied the existence of angels as well as the resurrection (Acts 23:8). But it has disturbed believers over the years. If there is no marriage—no sexual relationships—in our resurrection life, then won't that life be less than what we have now? What would life be like without the most intimate of relationships? The Bible does not directly answer this question since the answer should be obvious: we will have such a great capacity for intimacy with Christ and each other in our resurrection life that sexual intimacy will no longer be necessary![2] Besides, the Sadducees' concern in their question is "not about the mutual affection and companionship of husband and wife, but about *how to fulfill the command to have a child*, that is, how in the future life the family line will be kept going."[3]

The second key point Jesus makes goes beyond his direct response to the Sadducees' foolish question. It is a great affirmation that God is the God of the living, not the dead. Jesus makes this point by citing the statement God made to Moses as recorded in Exodus 3:6. When God said to Moses, "I am...the God of Abraham, the God of Isaac and the God of Jacob," he was speaking of men who had died hundreds of years prior to his statement. God is referring to them as alive to him. D. A. Carson observes: "[God] always loves and blesses his people; therefore it is inconceivable that his blessings cease when his people die."[4]

Romans 14:9 takes this a step further, claiming Jesus's death and return to life show that he himself is Lord both of the dead and of the living. His resurrection testifies to the truth of what he proclaimed to the Sadducees about God. As the God-man, Jesus's experience has demonstrated that God's blessings to his people do not stop when they die. Because of Jesus's resurrection, then, I can rejoice and have confidence about my future life after I die. I take to heart what the apostle Paul writes in 1 Corinthians 13:12: "For now we see only a reflection as in a mirror; then we shall see face to face. Now I know in part; then I shall know fully, even as I am fully known."

43

Jesus was raised from death . . .

To Confirm His Words about Being Raised to Life

> The angel said to the women, "Do not be afraid, for I know that you are looking for Jesus, who was crucified. He is not here; he has risen, just as he said. Come and see the place where he lay. Then go quickly and tell his disciples: 'He has risen from the dead and is going ahead of you into Galilee. There you will see him.' Now I have told you."
>
> Matthew 28:5–7

Christianity rises or falls on the truthfulness of its founder, Jesus the Messiah. According to the angel who spoke to the two women when they came to Jesus's tomb at dawn on the first day of the week, "He has risen, just as he said." Throughout his earthly ministry, Jesus predicted his death and resurrection. We can track these predictions in Matthew's Gospel.

Matthew 16:21 offers the following report, linking it to Peter's identification of Jesus as "the Messiah, the Son of the living God" (v. 16):

> From that time on Jesus began to explain to his disciples that he must go to Jerusalem and suffer many things at the hands of the elders, the chief priests and the teachers of the law, and that he must be killed and on the third day be raised to life.

Then, as Jesus was coming down from the mountain after his transfiguration, he instructed his disciples: "Don't tell anyone what you have seen, until the Son of Man has been raised from the dead" (17:9). Following this, Matthew 17:22–23 reports:

> When they came together in Galilee, he said to them, "The Son of Man is going to be delivered into the hands of men. They will kill him, and on the third day he will be raised to life." And the disciples were filled with grief.

Once more, Matthew 20:17–19 reports:

> Now Jesus was going up to Jerusalem. On the way, he took the Twelve aside and said to them, "We are going up to Jerusalem, and the Son of Man will be delivered over to the chief priests and the teachers of the law. They will condemn him to death and will hand him over to the Gentiles to be mocked and flogged and crucified. On the third day he will be raised to life!"

The Gospel of John contains a more cryptic prediction that the other three Gospels do not include. After Jesus cleared out the merchants and money changers from the temple courts in Jerusalem, people questioned his authority. John 2:19–22 records the conversation that followed:

> Jesus answered them, "Destroy this temple, and I will raise it again in three days."
> They replied, "It has taken forty-six years to build this temple, and you are going to raise it in three days?" But the temple he had spoken of was his body. After he was raised from the dead, his disciples recalled what he had said. Then they believed the scripture and the words that Jesus had spoken.

Irony and misunderstanding are prominent features in John's Gospel.[1] The people to whom Jesus spoke thought he was referring to the temple King Herod had begun rebuilding forty-six years before. Hundreds of stonemasons had worked on it. To think it could be destroyed and then rebuilt in three days was ridiculous. But Jesus was referring to himself. He was the replacement temple, the place where God's presence would dwell!

Significantly, after Jesus's resurrection, when the disciples recalled what he said, "they believed the scripture and the words that Jesus had spoken" (v. 22). If Jesus had not been raised from death to life, then his followers would have no reason to trust anything else he said. Whether his prediction had been downright deceitful or naive or simply wishful thinking, it would cast doubt on the truthfulness of anything else he said. But Jesus's resurrection means that we can trust his words and any other words recorded in Scripture.

So remember that Jesus "has risen, just as he said" when you wonder if he is really with you as he promised (Matt. 28:6). Remember that

Jesus "has risen just as he said" when you doubt his promise that God will take care of your needs for food and clothing if you seek first his kingdom (Matt. 6:31–33). Remember that Jesus "has risen, just as he said" when you question the reality of his coming "with power and great glory" (Matt. 24:29–31). Because Jesus rose from death just as he said, we can trust all of his words and his promises.

To Continue the Mission of God

> Then Jesus came to them and said, "All authority in heaven and on earth has been given to me. Therefore go and make disciples of all nations, baptizing them in the name of the Father and of the Son and of the Holy Spirit, and teaching them to obey everything I have commanded you. And surely I am with you always, to the very end of the age."
>
> Matthew 28:18–20

Jesus's final words at the end of Matthew's Gospel are known as the "Great Commission." This Great Commission is stunning for at least two reasons. First, it brings "the whole Gospel to a dynamic conclusion, which is in fact more a beginning than an end."[1] It is a "beginning" because it records Jesus's commission of his disciples to continue the mission of God. As the Father sent Jesus, now Jesus is sending his disciples (John 20:21). Second, this commission finds its basis in the resurrection of Jesus. This is clear from the way Matthew reports it immediately after finishing his report of Jesus's resurrection.

A closer look shows that the authority for this commission is linked to the resurrection. The resurrection has changed something regarding the authority of Jesus. But what? Matthew's Gospel has already emphasized Jesus's authority even prior to his resurrection. After Jesus finished delivering his Sermon on the Mount, "the crowds were amazed at his teaching, because he taught as one who had authority, and not as their teachers of the law" (Matt. 7:28–29). He declared and then demonstrated, by healing a paralyzed man, that "the Son of Man has authority on earth to forgive sins" (9:6). Jesus gave his twelve disciples "authority to drive out impure spirits and to heal every disease and sickness" (10:1). He even claimed that "all things have been committed to me by my Father" (11:27). Obviously, Jesus did not lack authority for his mission prior to his death and resurrection. So what has changed?

The key is the little word *all*—a word Jesus keeps repeating in his commission. Because of his death and resurrection, he now has "all

103

authority." As D. A. Carson observes, "the spheres in which he now exercises absolute authority are enlarged to include all heaven and earth."[2] This is an enormous result of the death and resurrection of Christ! "The Son becomes the one through whom *all* God's authority is mediated."[3] Here again is an allusion to the prophecy in Daniel 7:13–14 that the Son of Man "approached the Ancient of Days" and "was given authority, glory and sovereign power." Therefore, "the prophecy that the Son of Man would be enthroned as ruler of the world was fulfilled in the resurrection."[4]

When we, as Jesus's followers, go to "make disciples of all nations"—the main command in Jesus's commission—by leading them to Christ (signified by "baptizing") and building them up in Christ (signified by "teaching them to observe" what Jesus taught), we do so with the full authority of Christ behind us! As Christopher J. H. Wright says,

> The identity and the authority of Jesus of Nazareth, crucified and risen, is the cosmic indicative [statement of fact] on which the mission imperative stands authorized. . . . The limitations of Jesus's earthly ministry and the early mission trips of the disciples to the borders of Israel are now utterly removed. The Messiah is risen; the nations must hear and be drawn into covenant faith and obedience.[5]

This gives me a great sense of urgency and encouragement to continue the mission of Jesus. God did not place me on earth simply to have a family, enjoy a few hobbies, and work at a career. He has sent me here on a mission. Whether my vocation is in law enforcement, dentistry, accounting, or retail sales, my mission is to produce followers of Jesus Christ. Even my hobbies and relationships and life experiences are a means to this end. When people resist my pursuit of this mission and call me narrow-minded or fanatical, I keep on track by remembering that I am authorized to carry out the mission. The authority resides with the resurrected Lord, Jesus the Messiah.

To Share His Presence
with His Followers until His Return

> And surely I am with you always, to the very end of the age.
>
> Jesus (Matthew 28:20)

No adventure or mission can be successful without the presence of someone who has superior expertise, knowledge, or power. I cannot imagine hunting for elk in the mountains north of Yellowstone National Park without my friend Jason. I cannot imagine traveling to remote villages in southern Haiti and preaching there without respected Haitian pastor Jules. I cannot imagine upgrading my computer hardware and software without our office's IT specialist, Victoria. In the same way, I cannot imagine making disciples without the presence of my Savior Jesus.

Jesus's Great Commission ends with his remarkable promise to be with his followers always as they carry out his mission—a promise that will be good through the very end of the age, when they experience life in his unfiltered presence in the new heaven and earth (Rev. 21:1–22:5).

This promise is especially significant for two reasons. First, it provides encouragement for carrying out Jesus's mission. No matter how difficult their task, Jesus's followers can count on the presence of their crucified and risen Lord. Second, the promise of Jesus's presence advances a key theme in the developing story of the Bible: the presence of God. This theme is prominent in Matthew. In fact, it even frames the entire gospel![1] The Gospel of Matthew begins with an angel promising the birth of Jesus, who would be called Immanuel—"God with us" (1:23). It ends with Jesus promising to be present with his followers throughout history (28:20).

Matthew's Gospel, of course, is part of a larger story. The story of the Bible is actually the story of God reestablishing his presence among his people. But wait—we have often been told that the Bible is the story of redemption. So which is it? Both. The Bible is the story of redemption *from* sin *to* life in God's presence.

The story of the Bible begins in Genesis 1–2 with God creating human beings to represent him and to enjoy and expand, or spread, his glorious presence.² But three chapters into the Bible, human beings rebel against God and are driven out from his presence (Gen. 3). God goes to work, though, to restore his presence. The call of Abraham in Genesis 12:1–3 is a key step in God's plan. Through Abraham, God will develop a great nation through which he will bless the earth. Then through Moses, who leads the developing nation out of slavery in Egypt and into the promised land of Palestine, God commands the building of a tabernacle. This tabernacle, or tent, is the place where God will reveal his presence to his people (Exod. 25:8–9; 40:34–38). While no structure can ever contain God's presence (1 Kings 8:27; Isa. 66:1–2; Acts 17:24–25), God in his grace chose to live among his people for a time through the tabernacle and the ark of the covenant it housed (Exod. 25:33; 30:6).

The story continues with the coming of Jesus, who would be called *Immanuel*, "God with us" (Matt. 1:23). Jesus is the God-Man who "tabernacled" among his people (John 1:14) and presented himself as the replacement temple (2:13–25). But his resurrection signaled a new change in God's plan to live among his people. Jesus's final words recorded in Matthew's Gospel assure his people of his ongoing presence. Yet, this presence will be mediated through the Holy Spirit. The apostle Paul can speak of "Christ in you" precisely because "the Spirit of him who raised Jesus from the dead is living in you" (Rom. 8:11).

I am so thankful that I do not have to go on my mission for God alone. Jesus himself is with me as I work to introduce people to him and to train them to follow him. Until the day when the risen, exalted Christ returns to give me life in his unfiltered presence, I have confidence that the risen Christ is living in me—today and every day!

To Teach More about the Kingdom of God

> After his suffering, he presented himself to them and gave many convincing proofs that he was alive. He appeared to them over a period of forty days and spoke about the kingdom of God.
>
> Acts 1:3

The groups or movements to which we belong give us identity, opportunity, and security. My friends who are alumni of the University of Illinois proudly proclaim this at football games when they chant: "ILL, INI." So do my relatives a couple states east when they chant: "We are . . . Penn State." I have other friends who are quite invested in either the Girl Scouts or the Boy Scouts. And as a fly fisherman, I am glad to belong to a conservationist organization known as Trout Unlimited. But the greatest cause or movement to which anyone can ever belong is the kingdom of God.

An often-overlooked benefit of Jesus's resurrection is that it gave him an opportunity to provide more teaching about the kingdom of God. This is the central theme of Jesus's preaching and teaching *before* his death and resurrection. He announces to people in Capernaum: "I must proclaim the good news of the kingdom of God to the other towns also, because that is why I was sent" (Luke 4:43). Even the apostle Paul's preaching and teaching also finds its center in the kingdom of God (Acts 19:8; 20:25; 28:23, 31).

What is the kingdom of God? It is God's reign as king that restores life to all it was meant to be.[1] Jesus taught that "the Kingdom of God is of inestimable value and is to be sought above all other possessions"[2] (Matt. 6:33; 13:44–46). He taught that people can enter the kingdom only through new birth, a gift of God received through faith (John 3:3, 5, 8, 15–18).

Jesus also taught a "mystery"—that the future kingdom has arrived in advance to work within human beings (Matt. 13:1–52; Mark 4:1–32). "The time has come," he said. "The kingdom of God has come near. Repent and believe the good news!" (Mark 1:15). Jesus also said, "But if it is by the Spirit of God that I drive out demons, then the kingdom of God has come upon you" (Matt. 12:28). Yet Jesus also taught his disciples to pray "Your kingdom come" (6:10). On the night before his crucifixion, he told his disciples: "Truly I tell you, I will not drink again from the fruit of the vine until that day when I drink it new in the kingdom of God" (Mark 14:25). It is an inheritance only those who have done God's will can one day enter (Matt. 7:21–23; 25:34). So did the kingdom of God arrive with the coming of Jesus? The answer is "already, but not yet." It is both a present and future reality.

But what did Jesus speak about the kingdom of God *after* his resurrection when he appeared to his followers over a period of forty days? According to Acts 1:6–8, when asked if he was going to restore the kingdom to Israel "at this time," Jesus taught his followers not to worry about "the times or dates the Father has set by his own authority." Instead, he instructed his followers to use the time prior to the restoration of the kingdom to be his witnesses to the ends of the earth.

Furthermore, we can assume that what Jesus taught about the kingdom of God between his resurrection and ascension shows up in the teaching of the apostles in the New Testament. We learn much about the kingdom of God in the New Testament letters. We learn that the kingdom is a matter of "righteousness, peace and joy in the Holy Spirit" (Rom. 14:17). We also learn that even though the kingdom of God involves suffering (2 Thess. 1:5; Rev. 1:9), it is a matter of power (1 Cor. 4:20), it cannot be shaken (Heb. 12:28), and it is eternal (2 Pet. 1:11; Rev. 11:15).

Thank God that Jesus's resurrection enabled him to give a more complete picture of the greatest movement and cause to which we could ever belong—the glorious kingdom of God!

Jesus was raised from death . . . **47**

To Prove God's Commitment to Justice

> For he has set a day when he will judge the world with justice by the man he has appointed. He has given proof of this to everyone by raising him from the dead.
>
> Acts 17:31

My friend Roberto tells me disturbing stories about a violent drug cartel in his hometown in Mexico. The Zetas are a group founded by deserters of the Mexican Army Special Forces. Corrupt politicians and law enforcement officials have joined their ranks. The Zetas harass, extort, kidnap, and assassinate business leaders. Roberto fears for his own mother since upstanding citizens and children often get caught in the crossfire.

How can a loving God allow this? For that matter, if God exists, then why does he allow child abuse, sex trafficking, and massive starvation throughout the world? The resurrection of Jesus Christ proves God's intent to judge the world with justice. The apostle Paul made this point when he preached to the philosophers in Athens. It is for this reason that people everywhere should repent; that is, turn from their sin to God (Acts 17:30). Otherwise, they will face the fury of justice from the resurrected Christ, the one God has appointed to administer his justice.

Revelation 19 provides a vivid image of the resurrected Christ on the day he judges the world with justice. This description uses apocalyptic language—a type of language that works like a modern-day political cartoon. The details are symbolic, but they speak of a literal event. Here is the stunning description:

> I saw heaven standing open and there before me was a white horse, whose rider is called Faithful and True. With justice he judges and wages war. His eyes are like blazing fire, and on his head are many crowns. He has a name written on him that no one knows but he himself. He is dressed in a robe dipped in blood, and his name is the Word of God.

The armies of heaven were following him, riding on white horses and dressed in fine linen, white and clean. Coming out of his mouth is a sharp sword with which to strike down the nations. "He will rule them with an iron scepter." He treads the winepress of the fury of the wrath of God Almighty. On his robe and on his thigh he has this name written: KING OF KINGS AND LORD OF LORDS. (vv. 11–16)

This imagery is terrifying and may strike us the wrong way. Was Jesus really raised to do such violence? Yes. For God to bring about true justice and restore all relationships to what he designed them to be, there must be "the final exclusion of everything that refuses to be redeemed by God's suffering love."[1] But "should not a loving God be patient and keep luring the perpetrator into goodness?"[2] Yes, and this is exactly what God does by calling people everywhere to repent. Yet we must ask how patient God should be. Miroslav Volf answers:

> The day of reckoning must come, not because God is too eager to pull the trigger, but because every day of patience in a world of violence means more violence and every postponement of vindication means letting insult accompany injury.[3]

Here God's justice becomes deeply practical, affecting the way we respond to others. Deep reflection on God's intent to judge the world with justice by the man he appointed and raised from the dead (Acts 17:31) can actually help us escape the vicious cycles of retaliation in which we get caught. How can we expect people not to retaliate when their cities have been leveled, homes have been burned, wives and daughters and sisters have been raped, and the throats of fathers and sons and brothers have been slit? It is because Christ has absorbed God's violence against this evil through his death and, because he was raised, will destroy all who refuse to turn from this violence to God. We can only practice nonviolence and overcome evil with good when we believe in divine vengeance and leave room for it (Rom. 14:17–21).

The resurrected Christ is the one who will bring this justice. We long for his judgment because it will bring peace and restore our relationships to what God designed them to be. The peace justice brings is more than the absence of war. "It means *complete* reconciliation, a state of the fullest flourishing in every dimension—physical, emotional, social, and spiritual—because all relationships are right, perfect, and filled with joy."[4]

To Make Possible
the Judgment of the Wicked

Do not be amazed at this, for a time is coming when all who are in their graves will hear his voice and come out—those who have done what is good will rise to live, and those who have done what is evil will rise to be condemned. By myself I can do nothing; I judge only as I hear, and my judgment is just, for I seek not to please myself but him who sent me.

Jesus (John 5:28–30)

I have the same hope in God as these men themselves have, that there will be a resurrection of both the righteous and the wicked.

Acts 24:15

Then I saw a great white throne and him who was seated on it. The earth and the heavens fled from his presence, and there was no place for them. And I saw the dead, great and small, standing before the throne, and books were opened. Another book was opened, which is the book of life. The dead were judged according to what they had done as recorded in the books. The sea gave up the dead that were in it, and death and Hades gave up the dead that were in them, and each person was judged according to what they had done. Then death and Hades were thrown into the lake of fire. The lake of fire is the second death. Anyone whose name was not found written in the book of life was thrown into the lake of fire.

Revelation 20:11–15

You may be surprised to learn that those who believe in Jesus Christ are not the only ones who will experience resurrection in their future. Jesus made this clear when talking about those who heard his voice—the voice of the Son of God and Son of Man (John 5:25–27). These people will hear Jesus's voice and live because of their belief in him (v. 24). But another group will be raised too. Those who have done evil will rise from their graves to be condemned. Jesus assures his listeners that this judgment will be completely just since he bases it on the words and desire of his Father who sent him. Now, all this can only be possible if Jesus has been raised from death. Without his resurrection, he could not be this Son of Man who has the authority to judge and establish an eternal kingdom (Dan. 7:13–14).

Likewise, the apostle Paul said, "there will be a resurrection of both the righteous and the wicked" (Acts 24:15). Notice that this is the content of his hope in God.

The most vivid description of this judgment occurs in Revelation 20:11–15. In describing this vision, John does not identify the one seated on the throne. Presumably, it is God the Father, the "Ancient of Days" (Dan. 7:9; Rev. 19:4; 21:5). But Christ certainly occupies this throne too since the book of Revelation also describes him as standing in the center of God's throne (5:6) and sharing it with God (22:1).[1] The judgment is based on what is recorded in the books. This is certainly an allusion to the books in Daniel 7:10, which are associated with judgment, and the book in Daniel 12:1–2, which is associated with the deliverance of God's people.[2] Again, the vision uses symbolic language to speak of a literal reality. G. K. Beale explains that "the record books are metaphorical for God's unfailing memory, which at the end provides the account of the misdeeds of the wicked to be presented before them."[3]

But even this terrifying passage contains a ray of hope. Ultimately, banishment to eternal punishment happens to those whose names are not found in another book—the Book of Life. Those whose names are in the Book of Life will live forever in God's restored creation (Rev. 21:7). Getting one's name written in the Book of Life is not a matter of good works but a matter of receiving God's gift of eternal life through faith in Jesus Christ—the one who died for our sins and was raised to life (John 3:16; Rev. 21:6–7).[4]

You and I will be raised one day. That is for sure. Whether we are raised to life in God's presence or raised to face God's judgment depends on our response to God's Son, the Lord Jesus Christ, in this life. No wonder we stand fast in the gospel. No wonder we approach the task of proclaiming the gospel with a sense of urgency. People's eternal destinies are at stake.

To Give Him
Complete Supremacy

And he is the head of the body, the church; he is the beginning and the firstborn from among the dead, so that in everything he might have the supremacy.

Colossians 1:18

Grace and peace to you from him who is, and who was, and who is to come, and from the seven spirits before his throne, and from Jesus Christ, who is the faithful witness, the firstborn from the dead, and the ruler of the kings of the earth.

Revelation 1:4–5

Supremacy is a huge issue in our culture. Only one candidate gets elected to serve as president of the United States. Only one nominee wins the Golden Globe Award for Best Actress. Only one team wins the Super Bowl. Of course, presidents come and go. Award-winning actresses come and go. So do Super Bowl champions. Only one person in the universe remains supreme, and his supremacy stems from his resurrection! This person is, of course, Jesus Christ.

Both Paul and John use the image of ancient inheritance laws to help us grasp the staggering effect of Jesus's resurrection that we describe with the word *supremacy*. Both apostles describe Jesus as "the firstborn from the dead." The term *firstborn* does not at all imply that Jesus was a created being who had a beginning. Paul makes this clear a few sentences earlier when he describes Jesus as the "firstborn over all creation" and then immediately qualifies this by describing Jesus as the creator of all things, in heaven and on earth (Col. 1:15–16).

The term *firstborn* frequently appears in the Old Testament to describe priority and rank in families.[1] In Psalm 89:27, the term is applied to the line of David whose reign will be exalted forever. As the "firstborn from the dead," Jesus is the founder and exalted ruler of a new humanity—the first of all those who will be raised from death.

The result of this, according to both Paul and John, is his supremacy. In Colossians 1:18, "firstborn from among the dead" occurs as the last of three descriptions, thus putting it as the climax. It is immediately followed by a purpose statement: "so that in everything he might have the supremacy." The term *supremacy* has to do with being first or having first place. Christ's resurrection, then, resulted in him having first place in the universe that he, of course, created in the first place.

Revelation 1:4–5 also sees supremacy as the result of Christ's resurrection. Here, "the firstborn from the dead" is followed by another phrase that describes the logical outcome: "the ruler of the kings of the earth." Jesus could not be described this way if he had not been raised from death! Then a stunning image of Jesus's supremacy appears in the first vision John records in the book of Revelation. According to Revelation 1:13–16, John sees:

> Someone like a son of man, dressed in a robe reaching down to his feet and with a golden sash around his chest. The hair on his head was white like wool, as white as snow, and his eyes were like blazing fire. His feet were like bronze glowing in a furnace, and his voice was like the sound of rushing waters. In his right hand he held seven stars, and coming out of his mouth was a sharp, double-edged sword. His face was like the sun shining in all its brilliance.

John's response is not surprising. "When I saw him, I fell at his feet as though dead" (Rev. 1:17). But the risen Lord of glory placed his hand on John and said: "Do not be afraid. I am the First and the Last. I am the Living One; I was dead, and now look, I am alive for ever and ever!" (vv. 17–18). This is simply staggering! We do not serve the third or fifth greatest being in the universe. We do not serve one whose supremacy will end when he retires or when a greater being appears on the scene. Thanks to the resurrection, the Lord we serve is supreme over all. In him, all things hold together (Col. 1:17)—your cardiovascular system, the water cycle, the institution of marriage, and everything else we depend on for life. Like the sun at the center of the solar system, the glory of the risen Lord holds together all the aspects of our life, which revolve around it![2]

50

To Provide Life in the Unfiltered Presence of God

And I heard a loud voice from the throne saying, "Look! God's dwelling place is now among the people, and he will dwell with them. They will be his people, and God himself will be with them and be their God. 'He will wipe every tear from their eyes. There will be no more death' or mourning or crying or pain, for the old order of things has passed away."

Revelation 21:3–4

I did not see a temple in the city, because the Lord God Almighty and the Lamb are its temple.

Revelation 21:22

Then the angel showed me the river of the water of life, as clear as crystal, flowing from the throne of God and of the Lamb.

Revelation 22:1

I have seen some amazing sights during my lifetime. I will never forget watching the sun rise over the Great Plains as I climbed up the home stretch of Long's Peak, one of the tallest mountains in Colorado at 14,256 feet. I will never forget watching the sun set over the old city of Jerusalem from my vantage point on the Mount of Olives. But these sights pale in comparison to the final, astonishing vision recorded by the apostle John at the end of Revelation. This vision gives us a glimpse of the new life to which we will be raised to live in the new heaven and new earth. Once again, the resurrection of Jesus Christ is responsible for this. All the magnificent blessings of the new creation in this vision, recorded in Revelation 21:1–22:5, are possible because of the presence of the crucified and risen Messiah, the Lion of Judah who is also the Lamb![1]

Quite frankly, a lot of our visions of life in the new heaven and earth are boring. Popular pictures of heaven include people playing harps, wearing white robes, floating on clouds, and sporting halos around their heads. Or we envision heaven as a retirement home, or, worse yet, as an unending church service. But N. T. Wright observes this about Revelation 21:1–22:5: "We glimpse not a static picture of bliss, but a new creation bursting with new projects, new goals, and new possibilities."[2]

Life on the new earth in the new Jerusalem is the life you have always wanted—without the tears, death, mourning, crying, and pain that make life miserable (Rev. 21:4). This is possible because it is life in "the unfiltered presence of God." At last, "God's dwelling place is now among the people, and he will dwell with them. They will be his people, and God himself will be with them and be their God" (v. 3). Previously, no one could see God's face and live (Exod. 33:20; John 1:18). But now, God's people will see his face (1 John 3:2; Rev. 22:4) and experience the full, massive dose of his glory!

There will be no temple in the city "because the Lord God Almighty and the Lamb are its temple" (Rev. 21:22). That's stunning, because a temple was the place where God chose to reveal himself and dwell among his people on earth. By saying that the Lamb—the resurrected Messiah and Lord—is the temple, the vision communicates that there are no barriers to shield God's people from his full presence. This is paradise restored! A river runs through it, flowing with the water of life. The tree of life flourishes along both its banks. The garden of Eden has been reestablished, although this time it "encompasses the entire geography of the new creation."[3]

Now what will God's people do in this paradise? They will serve him (Rev. 22:3) and reign as kings (v. 5). This ruling takes place over the new creation, much like Adam was to do over the original creation as the "image of God." Imagine your work—creating, designing, writing, researching, recording, building—in a life minus all the frustrations and heartaches!

We need this vision when we have to face what life dishes out to us—everything from the mundane to the frustrating to the devastating. After talking about the glories of our future existence, C. S. Lewis wisely observed, "Meanwhile the cross comes before the crown and tomorrow is a Monday morning."[4] We can face Mondays because of what Jesus did on Friday and Sunday. His death and resurrection make possible our resurrection to new life in God's restored creation. May that hope purify us and make us more effective in living the resurrection life now as we wait for Christ's return!

Conclusion

A Final Question and a Tremendous Story

I hope this journey through *Risen* has impacted your life as deeply as it has mine. I have a question to ask you before you set this book down or put it back on the shelf. The question is: Have you responded to the gospel of Jesus Christ? Have you ever turned from your sin to embrace the good news that (1) Christ died for our sins according to the Scriptures, and (2) he was raised on the third day?

Remember, the apostle Paul is adamant in 1 Corinthians 15:2 that it is "by this gospel you are saved." Saved from what? Saved from God's judgment and wrath for our sin. Saved from an empty way of life in which we try to find love, joy, peace, significance, and meaning in anything and everything apart from the presence of God.

Let me help you understand the wonder of the gospel by briefly sketching the storyline to which it is connected. The Bible claims to be a book from God. Even though it was written over hundreds of years by many different authors, these authors "spoke from God as they were carried along by the Holy Spirit" (2 Pet. 1:21; see also 2 Tim. 3:16). As I suggested earlier, we can summarize the storyline of the Bible in a single sentence. The story of the Bible is *the story of God reestablishing his presence among his people.* The story unfolds in four basic movements, and you can remember it with these four words:

- Creation
- Fall
- Redemption
- Restoration[1]

The story begins with *creation*. According to the first two chapters of the Bible, Genesis 1 and 2, God created human beings to enjoy life in his presence and to display his wonder and beauty. It was the life we all want—a world of peace and justice, without death, disease, or conflict.

But just three chapters into the Bible, in Genesis 3, we learn human beings lost that world because of the *fall*. Both human beings and the creation lost the presence of God and fell into bondage because the first human beings turned from God. "Sin unleashed forces of evil and destruction so that now 'things fall apart' and everything is characterized by physical, social, and personal disintegration."[2] The Bible makes it clear that every person born into this world is guilty of sin because of our connection to Adam, the first human being. Romans 5:12 says that "sin entered the world through one man, and death through sin, and in this way death came to all people, because all sinned."

Thankfully, God did not wipe out all human beings and start over or give up on his plan to give human beings life in his presence. The bulk of the Bible's story is the story of *redemption*. This is God's saving work of delivering people from bondage to sin and restoring life in his presence. In Genesis 12, God took a pagan from the ancient Near East—Abram, later renamed Abraham—and promised to develop through him a nation to bless the earth.[3] That nation, Israel, eventually settled in Palestine, or what is modern-day Israel. Eventually a Savior, Jesus, was born to a Jewish virgin named Mary. Jesus was no ordinary savior. He was fully God and fully human! Because he was God, he had the power to save. Because he was human, he could take upon himself the punishment that all other human beings deserve. Jesus, the promised Messiah, or Christ, himself a descendant of Abraham, died as a victim of injustice and as our substitute, bearing the penalty of our evil and sin on himself. Then, as we have learned in this little book, he was raised to life on the third day after his death.

Because of Jesus's death and resurrection, we can look forward to the *restoration* of life in the presence of God. Jesus's death and resurrection "enable him to some day judge the world and destroy all death and evil without destroying us."[4] Then we will live forever in a life of beauty, intimacy, and adventure in the presence of God and his Son, Jesus Christ.

This is a tremendous story. Again, my question is, are you connected to it? Many people ignore the story and try to find love, joy, peace, significance, and meaning in smaller stories. These smaller stories may involve the misuse of God's good gifts and take the form of having an affair or embezzling money. These smaller stories may simply be an exclusive focus on playing golf, raising children, mountain biking, starting a business, pursuing a musical career, earning a master's degree, or whatever. But even the good stories are not enough. They only have meaning when we bring them into the larger story of God working to reestablish his presence among his people.

The Bible makes it clear that we receive God's salvation from sin and from an empty way of life through faith or belief. Ephesians 2:8–10 says it so clearly:

> For it is by grace you have been saved, through faith—and this is not from yourselves, it is the gift of God—not by works, so that no one can boast. For we are God's handiwork, created in Christ Jesus to do good works, which God prepared in advance for us to do.

Likewise, Romans 10:9 says: "If you declare with your mouth, 'Jesus is Lord,' and believe in your heart that God raised him from the dead, you will be saved." *Faith*, or belief, is reliance, trust, and dependence. Putting your faith in the crucified and resurrected Lord connects you to Christ and to all the benefits of God's salvation. Some passages in the Bible add another term to faith. It is the term *repentance*. For example, Jesus told people to "repent and believe the good news" (Mark 1:15). Repentance is a change of mind that results in a change of direction. Rather than continuing to pursue sin, you make a "U-turn" and run to Christ. Repentance does not mean that you will never sin again. It does mean "that we will no longer live at peace with our sin."[5]

So what are you waiting for? If you are convinced of your sin and convinced that Jesus Christ was crucified and raised to save you from your sins and from an empty way of life, then respond to the good news by repenting and believing. Remember, receiving God's salvation is based on what God did for you, not on what you do for God. It is not by works, so that you cannot boast in your own efforts.

No one is saved by praying a prayer. But a prayer is the usual way we express our faith. So talk to God and tell him that you recognize your sinfulness. Tell him that you are trusting only in the death and resurrection of Jesus Christ for salvation from sin's penalty and sin's power. Tell him now. "For, 'Everyone who calls on the name of the Lord will be saved'" (Rom. 10:13).

If you are someone who has put your faith in Jesus Christ—whether you took that initial step one minute ago, one year ago, or one decade ago—remember that you are "in Christ," that you have been raised with Christ, and that your life is now hidden with Christ in God (Col. 3:1–3). Live in this reality. Stand in it. For one day, when Christ appears, you will be raised to life to live with him in glory (v. 4)!

For Further Reading

Here are a few books I recommend to help in understanding the resurrection of Jesus Christ and the impact it has upon our lives.

Carson, D. A. *The God Who Is There: Finding Your Place in God's Story*. Grand Rapids: Baker Books, 2010.

Habermas, Gary R., and Michael R. Licona. *The Case for the Resurrection of Jesus*. Grand Rapids: Kregel, 2004.

Morrison, Frank. *Who Moved the Stone?* Reprint edition. Colorado Springs: Authentic Media, 2006.

Strobel, Lee. *The Case for Christ*. Grand Rapids: Zondervan, 1998.

Warnock, Adrian. *Raised with Christ: How the Resurrection Changes Everything*. Wheaton: Crossway, 2010.

Wright, N. T. *Surprised by Hope: Rethinking Heaven, the Resurrection, and the Mission of the Church*. New York: HarperOne, 2008.

Carson's volume, as the title suggests, will help you understand the storyline of the Bible. Few people understand it better than he does. The volumes by Habermas and Licona, Morrison, and Strobel all defend the validity of the resurrection as an historical event. Habermas has been researching, writing, and debating on the resurrection for years. Morrison's volume is a classic that was first published in 1930 and is still worth reading. Strobel, a former journalist and skeptic turned believer, devotes four chapters to "researching the resurrection." In these chapters, he interviews noted experts about the evidence for Jesus's resurrection. The volumes by Warnock and Wright explore how Jesus's resurrection impacts the way we live. Both are worth serious reflection for those who are serious about living cross-shaped and resurrection-shaped lives. Wright's volume is a more popular-level treatment of a massive study he published a few years ago: *The Resurrection of the Son of God* (Minneapolis: Fortress Press, 2003). The latter is a wonderful volume, but it is more technical than *Surprised by Hope*, and it tops out at 738 pages of text!

An Eight-Week Small Group Bible Study

This book can be used for an eight-week small group Bible study on the resurrection of Jesus Christ. Participants should read chapter 1 on the first day of the first class session. Then, if they continue reading one chapter each day and meet once a week, they will complete chapter 50 on session eight, the day their small group concludes the study. Each class session should focus on a key Bible passage or two from the previous week's chapters. I have provided a set of discussion questions for each session. Leaders can use some or all of them as they lead the discussion or teach a lesson. These questions are designed to encourage group members to dig into the biblical text. Some of the questions are answered in the chapters while others will require further reflection or study. For further resources, including commentaries on the Bible passages being studied, consult the endnotes.

Here is an example of how a small group Bible study could use this book. Suppose your small group or your Bible study meets on Tuesday evening. On the Tuesday evening you meet for session one, the leader will introduce the group to the study, teach a lesson or lead a discussion on John 11:17–44, and then read chapter 1 aloud to the group. Then, on Wednesday, group members will read chapter 2 on their own. On Thursday, they will read chapter 3 on their own. They will continue reading one chapter each day during the week. On the following Tuesday, group members will read chapter 8 prior to gathering for session two. They will continue this approach until the final Tuesday, when they read chapter 50 prior to gathering for the eighth and final session.

Session One

Assignment

Read chapter 1 during the group session. Then read chapter 2 the next day and continue reading at the rate of one chapter per day. Next week's assignment, then, is chapters 2–8.

Bible Passage

John 11:17–44

Discussion Questions

1. What did Martha believe about resurrection (John 11:24)? What opinions do people in our culture hold about the idea of resurrection?
2. How do we understand the apparent contradiction in Jesus's claim that believers die (John 11:25) and that believers will never die (v. 26)?
3. What do we learn about death from Jesus's anger (the meaning of "deeply moved in spirit" in John 11:33) and his weeping (v. 35)?
4. What is the significance of Jesus's miracle of raising Lazarus from death as the first half of John's Gospel (chaps. 1–12) moves toward its conclusion? How do we understand the contrast between the actions of Jesus in this miracle and the response of the religious leaders (John 11:45–53; 12:10–11)?
5. How does the story of Jesus raising Lazarus encourage us today when our loved ones die and when we face the reality of our own deaths?

Session Two

Assignment

Read chapters 2–8 prior to the group session.

Bible Passage

Acts 2:14–41

Discussion Questions

1. According to Acts 2:24, who raised Jesus from the dead, and what did this accomplish?
2. How does Psalm 16:8–11, quoted by Peter in Acts 2:25–28, defend the point Peter makes in Acts 2:25? See Acts 2:29–32 for clues as to the answer.
3. Peter describes the results of the resurrection of Jesus in Acts 2:33–36. What are these results?
4. What should people do as a result of the resurrection of Jesus (Acts 2:38–41)?
5. How prominent is the message of Jesus's resurrection in our presentation of the gospel and in the messages we hear in our churches? How much should we say about Jesus's resurrection when we proclaim the gospel of Jesus?

Session Three

Assignment

Read chapters 9–15 prior to the group session.

Bible Passage

Romans 8:9–25

Discussion Questions

1. According to Romans 8:11, who raised Jesus from the dead? How does this harmonize with what Peter says in Acts 2:24?
2. What is the effect of the Spirit's presence in believers' lives when they die (Rom. 8:11)?

3. What difference should the resurrection make in the way that we live (Rom. 8:12–13)?
4. What are some of the ways that Romans 8:14–25 describes our resurrection or life in our resurrected state?
5. How can the future resurrection of believers provide hope for you in your present sufferings?

Session Four

Assignment

Read chapters 16–22 prior to the group session.

Bible Passage

1 Corinthians 15:1–34

Discussion Questions

1. What are the basic elements of the gospel as described by 1 Corinthians 15:1–11? Go back to the Introduction or to chapter 19 for help with this.
2. How was Jesus raised according to the Scriptures (1 Cor. 15:4)? That is, how does the Old Testament point forward to Jesus's resurrection?
3. Does it really matter if the resurrection is true? If it is not, what do we lose according to 1 Corinthians 15:12–19? Furthermore, what enemies are destroyed as a result of the resurrection (1 Cor. 15:24–26)?
4. Does 1 Corinthians 15:29 encourage or endorse the practice of baptism for the dead? Why or why not?
5. How has this first half of the great resurrection chapter challenged you personally or as a group? What changes will you make in your beliefs or behaviors in light of its teaching about resurrection?

Session Five

Assignment

Read chapters 23–29 prior to the group session.

An Eight-Week Small Group Bible Study

Bible Passage

1 Corinthians 15:35–58

Discussion Questions

1. What are some examples from nature of how death has to occur to bring about life? What are some examples from nature of different kinds of physical bodies?
2. As believers in Jesus, how will our resurrection bodies be different from our current bodies (1 Cor. 15:42–49)? Related to this, what is the difference between a "natural body" and a "spiritual body"?
3. What will it mean for believers to "bear the image of the heavenly man" (1 Cor. 15:49) in our resurrected bodies? How does the teaching of Genesis 1:26–28 on creation in the image of God impact our understanding of what it means to "bear the image of the heavenly man"?
4. Immortality would be an awful misery rather than an incredible blessing if we were not changed but left in our current condition. Why is this so?
5. According to 1 Corinthians 15:58, how does the reality of resurrection change the way that we live and serve Christ in the present? How will you live and serve differently in the next week or month as a result of what you have learned from the latter half of this great resurrection chapter?

Session Six

Assignment

Read chapters 30–36 prior to the group session.

Bible Passage

Ephesians 1:15–23 and Philippians 3:10–11

Discussion Questions

1. In Ephesians 1:15–23, what is the connection between knowing God better and the resurrection of Jesus?

2. Where in your life do you need to experience the kind of power that God used to raise Jesus from death?
3. How do we know that the language in Philippians 3:11 does not express doubt as to whether or not believers in Jesus Christ will experience resurrection? What does the statement in verse 11 mean?
4. Why do we need a balance between experiencing the power of Christ's resurrection and sharing in his sufferings?
5. Do you have any examples of how you have known the power of Christ's resurrection in your life? In what kind of situations or circumstances have you experienced this resurrection power?

Session Seven

Assignment

Read chapters 37–43 prior to the group session.

Bible Passage

Colossians 3:1–17

Discussion Questions

1. How can Colossians 3:1 say that we as believers have been raised with Christ when our resurrection is clearly a future event?
2. What exactly does it mean to set our hearts and minds on things above (Col. 3:1–2)? According to Colossians 3:1 and 3:3–4, why are we to set our hearts and minds on things above?
3. How can Colossians 3:5 describe greed as idolatry? Isn't idolatry the worship of false gods? Isn't idolatry bowing down to a statue or figurine that represents a false god or even the living God?
4. According to Colossians 3:12–17, what kind of behavior flows from the lives of God's people who have set their hearts on things above?
5. How well are you and the people in your small group and your local church doing when it comes to acting in a way that is consistent with your status as those who have been raised with Christ? What changes do you need to make to bring your behavior in line with your status?

Session Eight

Assignment

Read chapters 44–50 prior to the group session.

Bible Passage

Matthew 28:1–20

Discussion Questions

1. How did Jesus's followers—the women and the disciples—respond to the report of Jesus's resurrection? What aspects of their response were appropriate or inappropriate?
2. How did the guards, chief priests, elders, and soldiers respond to this same report?
3. The religious leaders concocted a plan in an attempt to discredit the report that Jesus had risen. In what ways do people today try to discredit Jesus's resurrection? What were the motives then for discrediting the report? What are peoples' motives today for denying the truthfulness of Jesus's resurrection?
4. Notice the relationship between Jesus's resurrection and his Great Commission. What is the connection between these two events? How does Jesus's resurrection influence or impact his instructions to his disciples? What exactly is involved in carrying out this commission?
5. What difference will Jesus's resurrection make in the way you and the members of your local church carry out Jesus's Great Commission?

Acknowledgments

It takes a village to write a book. At least it seems that way to me. I have been blessed with family, friends, mentors, and colleagues who have helped me a lot along the way. This little volume is much better than it would have been without their input and encouragement.

To begin with, I need to thank John Piper, a pastor I have never met but whose ministry I have appreciated. The idea for my little book was conceived on April 2, 2010—Good Friday—when I was nearing the end of his little book *Fifty Reasons Why Christ Came to Die*. I had challenged the church I pastor to read it throughout the Lenten season and end it on the day before Easter Sunday. As I was reading Piper's volume on Good Friday morning, the thought struck me that I should write on Jesus's resurrection in the same way that John Piper wrote on Jesus's death—to unpack its significance in an accessible form, in fifty readings that could be read over fifty days. The reality of Christ's resurrection has become especially dear to me in recent years. It converges with some other biblical themes that have captured my heart: the new covenant, the new heart we have received, and the new heaven and earth. So I set aside my preparation for a Good Friday message for a couple of hours and focused on Easter. Thanks to my Bible software program, I came up with a preliminary list of "fifty reasons why Christ was raised from death" in three hours.

I am grateful to my mentor and friend Gerry Breshears for pushing me to clarify some of my thoughts and to address some additional issues I did not include in my first draft. Gerry is immersed in Scripture, and so I always take his input seriously.

Eugene Peterson and Barry Cooper both pointed out my overuse of exclamation marks in my first draft! All right, that last one was intentional. They gently reminded me that there are better ways to show my enthusiasm for the resurrection of Jesus.

My children and their spouses made a huge contribution by working together to proofread the entire manuscript in two days before I submitted it to Baker Publishing Group. So here is a "shout-out" to Manny and Erin DeAnda, Grant and Anna Vander Ark, Ben and Nicole Mathewson, and Luke Mathewson. I also want to thank Ben and Grant for proofreading and commenting on the manuscript at an earlier stage in the process.

I am grateful to Craig Blomberg for writing the foreword and for always taking time to answer my questions when I want to pick his brain about some aspect of New Testament scholarship.

Madison Trammel deserves a lot of credit for pressing me to answer the "so what" question, for pointing out some ways to make my chapter titles less "clunky," and for encouraging me to introduce each chapter in a more compelling way.

I want to thank Rick Chalupnik and Clay Edens, two members of our pastoral staff who have met with me weekly for preaching planning meetings. They've always sharpened my thinking about the biblical text on the weeks I am preaching, and some of these chapters grew out of sermons on resurrection texts I discussed with them.

I owe a great debt of gratitude to the elders I serve with at the Evangelical Free Church of Libertyville (Illinois). Serving with them has been one of my life's great blessings. They have been supportive of my writing habit and have challenged, helped, and encouraged me in so many areas of my life and ministry. This team consists of Tom Erickson, Joe Giovanetto, Jim Gruenewald, Curt Gustafson, Jerry Parker, and Todd Ronne.

I also want to express my love for my church family. The people who comprise the Evangelical Free Church of Libertyville encourage me more than they realize. I appreciate the church's heart for carrying out the Great Commission of our risen Lord. We do not do it perfectly, and we won't as long as the church has me as its pastor. But we do our best together to become a loving community of Christ followers in order to reach a culture in need of God's presence. I wrote this book with them in mind, and I look forward to reading it through with them. My editor, Robert Hosack of Baker Publishing Group, has been a great help at every point of the process. I appreciate Bob's persistence and support. Likewise, Lindsey Spoolstra (my project editor), Ruth Anderson, Paula Gibson, and the rest of the team at Baker have done a wonderful job in getting this book ready for publication.

Turning now to family members, I am blessed to have a mother, Ruth Mathewson, who prays for me consistently as I preach and teach Scripture. Even a decade after my father died, she is still going strong in the service of our risen Lord. Perhaps she will be able to use this book when she teaches her next ladies' Bible study!

I do not know where to begin in thanking my children and their spouses for their love and encouragement, as well as the interest they have taken in this project. They have been my biggest fans, but they keep me humble too. So, I offer my love and gratitude to my daughter Erin DeAnda and her husband, Manny; my daughter Anna Vander Ark and her husband, Grant; my son Ben Mathewson and his wife, Nicole; and my son, Luke. Oh yes, I am grateful to my first grandchild, Blake Vander Ark, for bringing his "Papa" so much joy. I pray that Blake will believe in and set his affections on our risen Lord when he is old enough to understand the good news of Jesus Christ. This is my prayer for future grandchildren with whom my children and the Lord choose to bless me! My children think I should thank our family dog, Titan, and our cat, Griz. But I will pass on doing that since I cannot figure out how they made any contribution to this book.

Of course, I want to express my love and affection for my wife Priscilla. As we near thirty years of marriage, "we're still having fun, and you're still the one." More importantly, we're still serving our risen Lord together. I am grateful for Priscilla's support, her prayers, and her commitment to the writing ministry that God has allowed me to have.

Above all, "I thank Christ Jesus our Lord, who has given me strength, that he considered me trustworthy, appointing me to his service" (1 Tim. 1:12). He continues to pour out his grace and mercy on me every day. To him be honor and glory forever.

Notes

Introduction

1. My esteemed Hebrew professor, Dr. Ron Allen, pointed out to me years ago that the burial of Jesus Christ is not so much an additional element of the gospel—as in death, burial, and resurrection—as it is a confirmation of Jesus's death. *See* Ronald B. Allen, *Lord of Psalm: The Messiah Revealed in the Psalms* (Portland: Multnomah Press, 1985), 36–37.

2. See Christopher Hitchens, *God Is Not Great: How Religion Poisons Everything* (New York: Hatchette Book Group, 2007), 63–71. The chapter title on page 63 is "The Metaphysical Claims of Religion Are False."

3. Ibid., 143.

4. Eckhart Tolle, *A New Earth: Awakening to Your Life's Purpose* (New York: Dutton, 2005), 295.

5. This quote appeared on a promotional cover placed over the book jacket of Tolle's *A New Earth*. The cover invited readers to join Oprah and Eckhart for a worldwide web event that ran every Monday night for ten weeks.

6. Deepak Chopra, *Reinventing the Body, Resurrecting the Soul: How to Create a New You*, reprint edition (New York: Three Rivers Press, 2010), 20.

7. N. T. Wright, *Surprised by Hope: Rethinking Heaven, the Resurrection, and the Mission of the Church* (New York: HarperOne, 2008), 26.

8. Adapted from Wayne Grudem, *Systematic Theology* (Grand Rapids: Zondervan, 1994), 608–9.

9. See chap. 11 for more on how biblical teaching about the resurrection differs from popular afterlife views of disembodied existence, becoming an angel, and reincarnation.

Chapter 1

1. *Braveheart*, directed by Mel Gibson (1995; Paramount Pictures, 2000), DVD.

2. Wright, *Surprised by Hope*, 45.

3. N. T. Wright uses this expression in *The Resurrection of the Son of God* (Minneapolis: Fortress, 2003), 30–31.

4. Blaise Pascal, *Pensées*, trans. A. J. Krailsheimer (New York: Penguin, 1995), 45. This quote appears in chapter X, section 148 (or section 428 in some editions).

Chapter 2

1. Douglas Moo, *The Epistle to the Romans*, The New International Commentary on the New Testament (Grand Rapids: Eerdmans, 1996), 378.

Chapter 5

1. The hymn is "It Is Well with My Soul," written by Horatio G. Spafford (lyrics) and Philip P. Bliss (music). The quoted section is stanza three.

Chapter 6

1. Thomas R. Schreiner, *Romans*, Baker Exegetical Commentary on the New Testament (Grand Rapids: Baker, 1998), 47–48.
2. Author's translation. See Moo, *Romans*, 46.
3. Moo, *Romans*, 49.

Chapter 8

1. Ibid., 377.
2. Wright, *Resurrection of the Son of God*, 253.

Chapter 9

1. Grant R. Osborne, *Romans*, The IVP New Testament Commentary (Downers Grove, IL: InterVarsity, 2004), 153.

Chapter 10

1. Grudem, *Systematic Theology*, 842.
2. Schreiner, *Romans*, 353.

Chapter 11

1. Wright, *Resurrection of the Son of God*, 256.

Chapter 13

1. C. S. Lewis, *The Weight of Glory: And Other Addresses* (New York: Harper-Collins), 30.
2. Ibid., 31.
3. Moo, *Romans*, 511.
4. Lewis, *The Weight of Glory*, 43.

Chapter 14

1. "Joy to the World," written by Isaac Watts (lyrics) and arranged by Lowell Mason.

Chapter 15

1. The image of sonship is applied to the nation of Israel as a whole in Exodus 4:22; Jeremiah 3:19; 31:9; and Hosea 11:1.

Chapter 16

1. F. F. Bruce, *The Epistle to the Hebrews*, The New International Commentary on the New Testament (Grand Rapids: Eerdmans, 1964), 174.
2. Peter T. O'Brien, *The Letter to the Hebrews*, The Pillar New Testament Commentary (Grand Rapids: Eerdmans, 2010), 277.
3. Ibid., 278.

Chapter 17

1. Jewish people use the term "Hebrew Bible" or "Jewish Bible" to express a corpus (collection of texts) that is self-standing. In other words, Jewish folks view their Scriptures as a complete Bible, whereas the Christian expression "Old Testament" suggests that this collection is part of a larger whole that includes the New Testament. The expression "Tanakh" is an acronym for the three main divisions of the Hebrew Bible: the *Torah* (Law), *Nevi'im* (Prophets), and *Kethuvim* (Writings). See Carol Hupping, ed., *The Jewish Bible: A JPS Guide* (Philadelphia: The Jewish Publication Society, 2008), 2–3.
2. Wright, *Resurrection of the Son of God*, 321.
3. Ibid.
4. Craig Blomberg, *1 Corinthians*, The NIV Application Commentary (Grand Rapids: Zondervan, 1994), 296.
5. Gordon D. Fee, *The First Epistle to the Corinthians*, The New International Commentary on the New Testament (Grand Rapids: Eerdmans, 1987), 727.

Chapter 18

1. The latter image comes from "Screen Door," a song by the late Rich Mullins, who applied it to faith without works.
2. Wright, *Surprised By Hope*, 292–93. This is from Wright's caricature—albeit an accurate one!—of a liberal pastor's approach to the resurrection of Jesus.

Chapter 20

1. Anthony C. Thiselton, *The First Epistle to the Corinthians*, The New International Greek Testament Commentary (Grand Rapids: Eerdmans, 2000), 1232.
2. For the view that both earthly rulers and demonic rulers are in view, see Blomberg, *1 Corinthians*, 63, and Thiselton, 1232–33.
3. Clinton E. Arnold, *Powers of Darkness: Principalities and Powers in Paul's Letters* (Downers Grove, IL: InterVarsity, 1992), 89–99 and esp. 90–91.
4. Ibid., 163.

Chapter 21

1. Thiselton, *First Epistle to the Corinthians*, 1300.
2. Fee, *1 Corinthians*, 806.
3. Thiselton, *First Epistle to the Corinthians*, 1301.

Chapter 22

1. Fee, *1 Corinthians*, 769.
2. See also 2 Corinthians 4:8–11, 6:4–10, and 12:10.

Chapter 23

1. Fee, *1 Corinthians*, 770–71.
2. Blomberg, *1 Corinthians*, 305.
3. Ibid.

Chapter 24

1. Fee, *1 Corinthians*, 786.
2. Thiselton, *First Epistle to the Corinthians*, 1279.
3. See Ibid. This is "multiple intimacy without promiscuity" (see John Eldredge, *The Journey of Desire* [Nashville: Thomas Nelson, 2000]), 141.

Chapter 25

1. Note that while some English translations use the word "likeness" in Romans 8:29 and in 1 Corinthians 15:49, the Greek term is *eikon*, that is, "image."

Chapter 26

1. Stephenie Meyer, *Twilight* (New York: Little, Brown, and Company, 2005), 476.
2. Wright, *Resurrection of the Son of God*, 357.
3. Fee, *1 Corinthians*, 803, fn 33.
4. Murray J. Harris, "2 Corinthians" in *The Expositor's Bible Commentary*, vol. 10 (Grand Rapids: Zondervan, 1976), 346.
5. Thiselton, *First Epistle to the Corinthians*, 1297. I have slightly changed the appearance of the type, removing some italics and substituting italics for bold print.
6. Wright, *Resurrection of the Son of God*, 358.

Chapter 27

1. The Hebrew text actually uses the expression "ten words" (Exod. 34:28; Deut. 4:13, 10:4).
2. John T. McNeill, ed., *Calvin: Institutes of the Christian Religion*, vol. 2 (Philadelphia: Westminster, 1960), 360. This is book II, chapter VII, section 12.

Chapter 28

1. A close reading of 1 Corinthians 12–14 reveals this problem.

Chapter 29

1. For the full range of possibilities as to what Paul's affliction was, see Murray J. Harris, *The Second Epistle to the Corinthians*, *The New International Greek Testament Commentary* (Grand Rapids: Eerdmans, 2005), 166–72
2. The words in quotation marks come from the hymn "Great Is Thy Faithfulness," written by Thomas O. Chisholm (lyrics) and William M. Runyan (music). The quoted section comes from stanza three.

Chapter 30

1. Frank Justus Miller and G. P. Gould, trans., *Ovid III: Metamorpheses, Books I–VIII*, third edition. Loeb Classical Library, no. 42 (Cambridge: Harvard University Press, 1977), 148–61. The "Echo and Narcissus" episode appears in book III. The scene where Narcissus sees his reflection on the pond appears on page 155.

2. Harris, "2 Corinthians," 351.

3. Harris, *The Second Epistle to the Corinthians*, 423. This, of course, raises the question of the extent or breadth of the atonement. Harris observes: "There is universalism in the scope of redemption, since no person is excluded from God's offer of salvation; but there is a particularity in the application of redemption, since not everyone appropriates the benefits afforded by this universally offered redemption" (Ibid.). D. A. Carson captures nicely the balance between biblical texts that emphasize that Christ died for all and those texts that emphasize he died for his people, the elect: "If one holds that the Atonement is sufficient for all and effective for the elect, then both sets of texts and concerns are accommodated" (*The Difficult Doctrine of the Love of God* [Wheaton: Crossway, 2000], 76).

Chapter 31

1. Peter T. O'Brien, *The Letter to the Ephesians*, The Pillar New Testament Commentary (Grand Rapids: Eerdmans, 1999), 133.

2. The emphasis and literal translation of the Greek text is mine.

Chapter 32

1. For example, Richard Dawkins describes God as "jealous and proud of it; a petty, unjust, unforgiving control freak; a vindictive, bloodthirsty ethnic cleanser; a misogynistic, homophobic, racist, infanticidal, genocidal, filicidal, pestilential, megalomaniacal, sadomasochistic, capriciously, malevolent bully" (*The God Delusion* [New York: Mariner, 2008], 51). Some of this anger is directed at the so-called god of the Old Testament. But Christopher Hitchens has a chapter in his book *God Is Not Great* titled "The 'New' Testament Exceeds the Evil of the 'Old' One," 109–22.

2. Miroslav Volf, *Exclusion and Embrace: A Theological Exploration of Identity, Otherness, and Reconciliation* (Nashville: Abingdon, 1996), 303.

Chapter 33

1. Peter T. O'Brien, *The Epistle to the Philippians*, The New International Greek Testament Commentary (Grand Rapids: Eerdmans, 1991), 412.

Chapter 34

1. This is suggested by a close reading of Colossians. See Arnold, *Powers of Darkness*, 139. David L. Mathewson, a professor of New Testament at Denver Seminary (and my brother!), recently did research on the "Colossian heresy" described in Colossians 2. After reading all of the non-Scriptural texts in the Dead Sea Scrolls, as well as other Jewish texts in the first century AD, he observed that all of the pagan magical practices referred to in Colossians were prevalent in first-century Judaism (personal correspondence, May 8, 2012).

2. Peter T. O'Brien, *Colossians, Philemon*, Word Biblical Commentary (Waco: Word, 1982), 133.

3. This view, known as Gnosticism, became fully developed a couple centuries after Paul's letter to the Colossians.

4. O'Brien, *Colossians, Philemon*, 52.

5. G. K. Beale, "Colossians," *Commentary on the New Testament Use of the Old Testament*, ed. by G. K. Beale and D. A. Carson (Grand Rapids: Baker, 2007), 856–57.

6. O'Brien, *Colossians, Philemon*, 53.

7. Arnold, *Powers of Darkness*, 144.

Chapter 35

1. Lewis, *The Weight of Glory*, 26.

2. O'Brien, *Colossians, Philemon*, 161.

3. Lewis, *The Weight of Glory*, 26.

4. Personal correspondence with Gerry Breshears, March 26, 2011.

5. O'Brien, *Colossians, Philemon*, 159.

Chapter 36

1. Grudem, *Systematic Theology*, 1092.

2. This expression is from a question Sam poses to Gandalf, in bewilderment and incredible joy when he discovers that Gandalf is alive and that the Darkness is being lifted: "Is everything sad going to come untrue?"

Chapter 37

1. O'Brien, *Colossians, Philemon*, 181. The definitions of the vices in these two lists come largely from pp. 181–88.

2. The term is used positively in Luke 22:15 where it refers to Jesus's desire to eat the Passover meal with his disciples before he suffered. It is also used by Paul in 1 Thessalonians 2:27 to describe his longing to see the members of the church in Thessalonica.

3. Even in the Old Testament, God warns his people about setting up idols in their hearts (Ezek. 14:3–4).

Chapter 38

1. I. Howard Marshall, *1 and 2 Thessalonians* (Vancouver: Regent College, 1983), 59.

2. G. K. Beale, *1–2 Thessalonians*, The IVP New Testament Commentary Series (Downers Grove, IL: InterVarsity, 2003), 62.

Chapter 39

1. See the outstanding treatment of the Bible's use of the shepherding image in Timothy S. Laniak, *Shepherds After My Own Heart: Pastoral Traditions and Leadership in the Bible*, New Studies in Biblical Theology (Downers Grove, IL: InterVarsity, 2006). For a more popular-level collection of reflections on the application of the shepherding metaphor to God, see Timothy S. Laniak, *While Shepherds Watch Their Flocks: Forty Daily Reflections on Biblical Leadership* (Matthews, NC: Shepherd Leader Publications), 2007.

2. My translation of the Hebrew text of Psalm 23:6. The Hebrew term traditionally translated as *follow* means to "pursue, chase, persecute." The goodness and loyal love of our Shepherd literally chases us down throughout our lives!

3. Gary M. Burge, *John*, The NIV Application Commentary (Grand Rapids: Zondervan, 2000), 143. Craig S. Keener, *The Gospel of John: A Commentary*, vol. 1 (Peabody, MA: Hendrickson, 2003), 604.

4. Burge, *John*, 143.

5. "Savior, Like a Shepherd Lead Us," by Dorothy A. Thrupp (lyrics) and William B. Bradbury (music).

Chapter 40

1. John Piper, *Finally Alive* (Fearn, UK: Christian Focus, 2009), 83.

Chapter 41

1. Christopher Parkening's remarkable story appears in his autobiography, written with Kathy Tyers, *Grace Like a River* (Carol Stream, IL: Tyndale House, 2006).

Chapter 42

1. D. A. Carson, *Matthew*, The Expositor's Bible Commentary, vol. 8 (Grand Rapids: Zondervan, 1984), 461.

2. As noted previously, one author describes this as "multiple intimacy without promiscuity" (Eldredge, *Journey of Desire*, 141).

3. Wright, *Resurrection of the Son of God*, 423.

4. Carson, "Matthew," 462.

Chapter 43

1. D. A. Carson, *The Gospel According to John*, The Pillar New Testament Commentary (Grand Rapids: Eerdmans, 1991), 182.

Chapter 44

1. R. T. France, *Matthew*, Tyndale New Testament Commentaries (Grand Rapids: Eerdmans, 1985), 411.

2. Carson, "Matthew," 594.

3. Ibid., 595.

4. Joachim Jeremias, *New Testament Theology: The Proclamation of Jesus* (New York: Scribner's, 1977), 310. Jeremias goes on to say that the disciples experienced Jesus's resurrection "not as a mighty act of God *in the course of* history hastening to its end (though this is what it must have seemed to them after a short interval), but as the dawn of the eschaton" (Ibid.). The term *eschaton* refers to "the end," that is, the final event in God's plan.

5. Christopher J. H. Wright, *The Mission of God: Unlocking the Bible's Grand Narrative* (Downers Grove, IL: InterVarsity, 2006), 60, 512.

Chapter 45

1. Craig L. Blomberg, *Matthew*, The New American Commentary (Nashville: Broadman, 1992), 433–34.

2. On the notion of the first humans being responsible to expand God's presence, see G. K. Beale, *The Temple and the Church's Mission: A Biblical Theology of*

the Dwelling Place of God, New Studies in Biblical Theology (Downers Grove, IL: InterVarsity, 2004), 81–87.

Chapter 46

1. George Eldon Ladd has provided this classic definition of the kingdom of God: "The Kingdom of God is the redemptive reign of God dynamically active to establish his rule among men, and that this Kingdom, which will appear as an apocalyptic act at the end of the age, has already come into human history in the person and mission of Jesus to overcome evil, to deliver men from its power, and to bring them into the blessings of God's reign" (*The Presence of the Future*, rev. ed. [Grand Rapids: Eerdmans, 2002], 218).
2. Ibid., 238.

Chapter 47

1. Volf, *Exclusion and Embrace*, 299.
2. Ibid.
3. Ibid.
4. Timothy Keller, *Generous Justice* (New York: Dutton, 2010), 174.

Chapter 48

1. Grant R. Osborne, *Revelation*, Baker Exegetical Commentary (Grand Rapids: Baker, 2002), 720.
2. G. K. Beale, *The Book of Revelation*, The New International Greek Testament Commentary (Grand Rapids: Eerdmans, 1999), 1032.
3. Ibid., 1033.
4. First John 5:4–5 makes it clear that being an overcomer is tied to faith. The one who overcomes is the one who believes that Jesus is the Son of God.

Chapter 49

1. O'Brien, *Colossians, Philemon*, 44.
2. This image comes from John Piper at a 2004 Desiring God Conference session.

Chapter 50

1. See Revelation 5 for the stunning image of the Lion of Judah who is also the Lamb of God who takes away the sin of the world and brings about God's purposes through his death.
2. Wright, *Resurrection of the Son of God*, 476.
3. Beale, *Revelation*, 1106.
4. Lewis, *The Weight of Glory*, 45.

Conclusion

1. I have adapted my summary of the Bible's story from a fine summary by Timothy J. Keller, "The Gospel in All Its Forms," *Leadership Journal* 29, no. 2 (Spring 2008): 78.
2. Ibid.

3. The name Abram means "exalted father," an ironic name given that Abram did not yet have any children as he entered the later years of his life. Yet God changed Abram's name to Abraham, "father of many," when Abraham was ninety-nine years old and was still childless. But the name change was made in anticipation of Abraham becoming the father of many nations. See Genesis 17:4–5.

4. Keller, "The Gospel in All Its Forms," 78.

5. Greg Gilbert, *What Is the Gospel?* (Wheaton: Crossway, 2010), 81.

Steven D. Mathewson has been serving as senior pastor of the Evangelical Free Church of Libertyville, Illinois, since 2006. He and his family moved to Chicagoland after twenty years in Montana. Steve is also an adjunct professor at Trinity Evangelical Divinity School and Moody Bible Institute. In addition, he teaches regularly in the doctoral program at Denver Seminary. His other books include *The Art of Preaching Old Testament Narrative* (Baker) and *Joshua-Judges* in *The People's Bible Commentary* (The Bible Reading Fellowship, Oxford, England).

Steve graduated from Multnomah University, Western Seminary (master's degree in Hebrew Bible), and Gordon-Conwell Theological Seminary (doctorate in preaching).

Steve is passionate about fly fishing and loves to fish for trout on the Madison and Yellowstone Rivers in Montana any time he gets the chance. He is an avid baseball fan and still roots for the St. Louis Cardinals even though he lives in Chicago Cubs country. When Steve is forced to stay indoors, he enjoys activities like studying the Dead Sea Scrolls or reading western novels by Louis L'Amour. Steve and his wife, Priscilla, miss watching their children compete in high school sports now that all four have graduated from high school.

To access the author's blog, find more resources related to this book, and learn about other books by Steve, visit www.StevenDMathewson .com and www.facebook.com/Risen.Steven.D.Mathewson.